# Carrying Them with Us

# Carrying Them with Us

## Living through Pregnancy or Infant Loss

David M. Engelstad and
Catherine A. Malotky

CARRYING THEM WITH US
Living through Pregnancy or Infant Loss

All biblical references in this book come from the New Revised
Standard Version.

An excerpt in chapter 3 is taken from "Persistent depressive disorder
(dysthymia)," Mayo Clinic, August 8, 2017, https://www.mayoclinic.
org/diseases-conditions/persistent-depressive-disorder/symptoms-
causes/syc-20350929. Used with permission of Mayo Foundation
for Medical Education and Research. All rights reserved.

An excerpt in chapter 4 is taken from Kathleen Sheeder Bonanno,
"What People Give You" from *Slamming Open the Door*. Copyright
© 2009 by Kathleen Sheeder Bonanno. Reprinted with the
permission of The Permissions Company, Inc., on behalf of
Alice James Books, www.alicejamesbooks.org.

Cover design: Rob Dewey

Print ISBN: 978-1-5064-2740-9
eBook ISBN: 978-1-5064-3417-9

The paper used in this publication meets the minimum
requirements of American National Standard for Information
Sciences — Permanence of Paper for Printed Library Materials,
ANSI Z329.48-1984.

Our three daughters have been the gift of a lifetime, and this book is especially dedicated to Erin, Cara, and Abbie, with deep gratitude for all you have taught us. Our life is graced.

# Contents

# Series Preface

MY MOST sincere wish is that the Living with Hope series will offer comfort, wisdom—and hope—to individuals facing life's most common and intimate challenges. Books in the series tackle complex problems such as addiction, parenting, unemployment, pregnancy loss, serious illness, trauma, and grief and encourage individuals, their families, and those who care for them. The series is bound together by a common message for those who are dealing with significant issues: you are not alone. There is hope.

This series offers first-person perspectives and insights from authors who know personally what it is like to face these struggles. As companions and guides, series contributors share personal experiences, offer valuable research from trusted experts, and suggest questions to help readers process their own responses and explore possible next steps. With empathy and honesty, these accessible volumes reassure individuals they are not alone in their pain, fear, or confusion.

The series is also a valuable resource for pastoral and spiritual care providers in faith-based settings. Parish pastors, lay ministers, chaplains, counselors, and other staff and volunteers can draw on these volumes to offer skilled and compassionate guidance to individuals in need of hope.

Each title in this series is offered with prayer for the reader's journey—one of discovery, further challenges, and transformation. You are not alone. There is hope.

Beth Ann Gaede, Series Editor

## Titles in the Living with Hope Series

*Nurturing Hope: Christian Pastoral Care in the Twenty-First Century* (Lynne M. Baab)

*Dignity and Grace: Wisdom for Caregivers and Those Living with Dementia* (Janet L. Ramsey)

*Jobs Lost, Faith Found: A Spiritual Resource for the Unemployed* (Mary C. Lindberg)

*They Don't Come with Instructions: Cries, Wisdom, and Hope for Parenting Children with Developmental Challenges* (Hollie M. Holt-Woehl)

*True Connection: Using the NAME IT Model to Heal Relationships* (George Faller and Heather P. Wright)

*Waiting for Good News: Living with Chronic and Serious Illness* (Sally L. Wilke)

*Carrying Them with Us: Living through Pregnancy or Infant Loss* (David M. Engelstad and Catherine A. Malotky)

*A Grief Received: What to Do When Loss Leaves You Empty-Handed* (JL Gerhardt)

*When Trauma Wounds: Pathways to Healing and Hope* (Karen A. McClintock)

*Addiction and Recovery: A Spiritual Pilgrimage* (Martha Postlethwaite)

# Preface

IF YOU have lost a child through miscarriage, at birth, or in early infancy, this book is for you. We have been there, and we know it is not an easy road. We hope this book will be helpful to you as you make your way from the intensity of the early days following the death of your child through the months and years that follow.

To read any book on grief takes some courage and trust. Will the authors be sensitive to your feelings and hold them gently? Will the authors take seriously the depth of your grief and not offer cheap advice, as if your grief could be easily "fixed"? This book has been guided by the importance of these questions and by the wisdom and promise of healing conveyed in Psalm 23, which speaks of walking "*through* the valley of the shadow of death." This book is intended to be a companion for you on this journey.

Our walk through this valley began when our firstborn twin, Erin, died at eight weeks of age. The coroner diagnosed SIDS (sudden infant death syndrome), because there was no apparent cause for her death.

On November 30, 1984, we had put both of our daughters back to sleep around 7:00 a.m. after an efficient but intense hour of feeding, changing, and comforting two babies. That morning, we hoped for one more opportunity for parental sleep before getting up for the day. We had just begun going to bed right after the supper hour, hoping to get eight hours of sleep in total, even if it came in one- to two-hour stretches. Nursing two babies every few hours through the night required both of us. Though Catherine was up first when a hungry baby cried, David wasn't far behind. As the first baby finished feeding, he got the second one up, changed her, and handed her over to be fed. Then he took over the first one and settled her to sleep while the second one nursed. He headed back to bed after the first one was down, and Catherine settled the second after she was finished nursing. Each feeding always seemed to end too close to the next wake-up call from a hungry twin.

We were exhausted and knew by eight weeks that we had to sleep more if we were going to be even halfway decent parents, so we decided that a wakeful baby would need to cry herself back to sleep once we made sure she was fed, changed, and calmed. That morning, after both babies had been fed, Erin was the wakeful one and cried heartily, but she eventually quieted, and we slept until we were awakened by a baby crying again at about 10:00 a.m.

We launched the routine: Catherine got up to nurse the crying baby, anticipating the heads-up to David to wake up the sleeping baby when it was almost time to switch them over. This time, it was Cara who woke up first. Before she got Cara up to nurse, Catherine gently touched Erin's sleeping head, remembering that she had cried herself to sleep a couple of hours earlier.

But Erin was not sleeping. She was cold. Catherine turned her over, and she was clearly dead, her body lifeless and pale. That began the nightmare no parent wants to face. Our baby had died.

This book is a reflection of what we have learned in the thirty-plus years since that fateful morning, and we hope it will be helpful to you as you navigate this painful terrain. Probably you, like us, were ready to joyfully commit love and effort to a relationship full of promise with this baby (in our case, two). As in a marriage, parents are prepared to honor the relationship with their children "for better or worse; for richer or poorer; in sickness and in health."

Though the next phrase in this traditional wedding vow is "until death do us part," we generally don't expect death to show up any time soon, in partnered or parental relationships. We parents know at some level that life is precarious for a baby-in-formation and for an oh-so-new infant. Yet we tend to be understandably preoccupied with the baby's utter dependence on us for care and nurture, both before and after birth. We may have fears about the baby, but most of us are not debilitated by anxiety. We focus more on the expected birth and the loving, cherishing, protecting, and nurturing to come. These commitments are rarely spoken out loud but exist as a deeply felt, determined pledge of parental love and support.

Infant death tramples these expectations into the dust. Children are supposed to bury their parents, not parents their children. A child's death leaves parents devastated and disoriented. A once-familiar world suddenly feels cold and capricious. Infant death is emotionally traumatic for parents, whether the death was sudden or not. Because the injuries of grief are less well known and harder to see, many grieving parents report feeling not just overwhelmed but also alone.

Rather than face the trauma, we might be tempted to leave behind the tragedy of an infant's death and charge into a future free of trauma and grief. Perhaps this is even possible, but the prerequisite for this outcome would be forgetting the child who died and forever blotting that life out of both heart and memory. You would also need to forget all these wonders:

- The joyful anticipation of pregnancy and parenting
- Your promise of lifelong love and commitment to your child
- The blessings of God, who formed you (the parents) and your child-in-the-making

Choosing this path of forgetting is not the way of healing, however. The healing path of grief instead requires remembering what remains:

- Your enduring love for the precious little one who died
- The commitment you made to be the child's parent
- The God who inspired this love and grieves with you

Jesus chose this second path as he entered into the final days of his life. In the Garden of Gethsemane, Jesus prayed, "If it is possible, let this cup pass from me; yet not what I want but what you want" (Matthew 26:39; Mark 14:36; Luke 11:42). He faced a different kind of trauma, but he chose to walk into the midst of it, to be conscious of what was happening to him, trusting that God could and would bring life out of death.

Few of us will have the trust that Jesus had. As bereaved parents, we are likely to doubt everything, especially our faith. But because Jesus trusted, we can still ask in our prayers, even when we feel full of doubt, "God, do not forsake us in this hour of need. Even when it feels like we are dying, help us trust you will bring us again to life." Through Jesus's life and death and resurrection, we see this promise incarnate: life will rise up out of death.

## In Faith

As we have just done, we will use language and metaphors of faith and spirituality as we talk about grief in this book—not exclusively, but often. We found the framework of our faith tradition to be very helpful as we grieved (and still grieve) our daughter's death. You may use different language to name your relationship with or understanding of a higher power. Our use of spiritual language is not intended to draw you away from the faith traditions you embrace. Our references are Christian because we are Christian. We hope that wherever you are in your faith journey, you will find some meaning in what we offer.

This book offers a spiritual perspective on grief. Grief certainly is a psychosocial, intellectual, and intensely emotional process. We propose that grief also deeply affects our spirituality. We define spirituality as the sum of your beliefs and experiences:

- What you call sacred
- How you experience a power greater than yourself (God)
- What you feel passionate about
- What you believe is true about humans and human nature
- How you think about good and evil
- What you see as just or unjust
- Your sense of awe and wonder

- Your convictions and commitments (including where they come from and what sustains them)
- Your capacity to heal, to trust, to hope
- Your instincts and intuition
- The way you love and allow yourself to be loved
- Your aspirations about what you want to do and be
- Your openness to forgive and to be forgiven
- Your imagination and creativity

Notice that our understanding of spirituality is not limited to the doctrines or teachings of any given religion. Rather, it offers a wellspring of resources to help us cope with grief, even as it is surely affected by grief.

Grief, seen through the lens of spirituality, opens into a future beyond the devastating sadness that marks the beginning of the grief journey. To be sure, the dislocation of grief must be tended with loving care and support. More than half of this book will focus on just that concern. Yet running alongside this concern is the theme of new life. Picture the aftermath of a forest fire's devastation, including the slow emergence of plant life from the ashes. New life is also slowly emerging in you from the ashes of your baby's death. We have written about both of these forces in this book, because we see them—we have experienced them—as powerfully present in grief.

## Our Intention

While we have learned from our journey and will share much of it in this book, we want to offer a look at grief that is broader than our own experience. Yet we also could not have written apart from our experience of Erin's death. In fact, writing this book has over and over again taken us back to her life and death. A deep sadness remains, even after all these years. Yet we also feel a mysterious sense of grace, for in writing this book, we get to parent her again. We can remember her with you, even as you are remembering your little one with us.

In his role as a hospital chaplain, David led a pregnancy and infant loss support group for more than a decade. The mothers and fathers who attended this support group shared stories that inform and enrich this book. While their stories had much in common, each parent's experience was also unique. Therefore, when you find something helpful in this book, something that you may have in common with these other mothers and fathers, embrace it and incorporate it into your life in any manner that works for you. And when any part of this book does not seem to address your story's uniqueness, feel free to ignore it.

We have also written with caregivers in mind and have devoted a section at the end of each chapter to people in this role. If you are a caregiver, we trust that you desire to expand your capacity to be empathetic and supportive. Since grieving parents often yearn for the refuge of family and friends, we have aimed to equip you to be a refuge for them in a manner that is mindful of your gifts and limits. We believe that better understanding grief also equips you to face other losses that you will one day encounter.

To write a book on pregnancy and infant loss is a humbling task, because we ourselves recall how no words were ever adequate to describe or make sense of it. Yet we also remember how, after our daughter died, we yearned for encounters (written or in person) that assured us that others who experienced a child's death have found a way to keep going.

No words or metaphors are ever equal to the task of capturing and honoring the essence of a beloved child who has died. We intend our words and your reading of them to be an act of remembering through which you hold your beloved child in your heart. Of course, you would love to hold them in your arms. We are so sorry that is not possible. This book was written in memory of your children and in honor of all whose hearts are full of love for them.

# Acknowledgments

WE ARE grateful to many for their support, both at the time we first walked through the valley of the shadow of death (Psalm 23:4 RSV) and now, in our writing of this book.

We are very aware that we would not have survived those early days without the love and care of the congregation we both served and called home, Our Saviour's Lutheran Church in South Minneapolis. We leaned on them and our colleagues there during difficult pregnancies (both for the twins and the subsequent pregnancy), and they were absolutely our rock when we were devastated by grief when Erin died. They wept with us in so many ways and were graciously able to both support us as young parents and welcome us as their pastors. In a time when "clergy couples" were still new, they were game—even enthused—to try.

The midwives and nurses in the midwife unit at Hennepin County Medical Center were so ahead of their time, and we relied on their expertise. Their sensitivity to our hopes for minimal intervention in spite of the higher risk of a twin pregnancy and their clear investment in our well-being after Erin's death was such a grace for us. Their expertise and compassion surrounded us again when our third daughter was born three years later. They knew our story and gave us space to hold both our grief and our joy together when she was born.

We are also deeply grateful for the good people at Minnesota Sudden Infant Death Center at Minneapolis Children's Hospital and the support groups for newly bereaved parents we attended in 1984–1985. We particularly appreciate the skillful leadership of Sharon Larson, whose care for us did not stop when we stopped coming to the group. She received our stricken phone call years later, after a report on the success of the Back to Sleep initiative, which had reduced SIDS deaths by nearly half. We had put our babies to sleep on their stomachs as a matter of course, which was even considered best practice then—until research and the decreasing rate of SIDS deaths proved otherwise.

We were blessed by the expertise of therapists. Janice Nadeau's skill as a grief counselor helped us live through those early days. And Robert Hurlbut, himself a bereaved father of twins (like us, he and his wife got to raise only one of them), helped us think about our marriage as grief invited us deeper into the soul work we needed to do.

And we cannot say enough about the generosity of the bereaved mothers and fathers who attended the pregnancy and infant loss support groups that David co-led for many years at Fairview Southdale Hospital, in addition to the bereaved parents we have had the privilege of serving as pastor. Their stories of grief and courage, their honesty and vulnerability with us are what inspired our desire to offer the unique perspective of our experience and theirs to others who are walking this difficult path. Though they are not named explicitly, their wisdom is the foundation for much of this book.

Our hearty thanks to Beth Gaede, a good and faithful editor, who has been serving the church and the gospel for so many years. She created a shame-free zone for us, asked good questions, and loved us and this book into a better place than where it began. We know it's her job. We know she's good at it. But our gratitude is profound. She trusted us to write and in so doing has helped us create something that feels like it belongs in our file marked "legacy."

Finally, we offer thanks to family (especially our daughters), colleagues, and friends, who have continued to support us over the years, who remember our loss, and who still, sometimes, receive our tears. They are God incarnate for us and a sure sign of God's redemptive grace at work. We are humbled and so very grateful.

# 1

## How Can This Have Happened?

IF YOUR baby has died, we are so sorry. How can this have happened? This is not how the story is supposed to end. Not so soon. Not at all.

We parents presume that our children will be born alive and healthy. And why shouldn't we? Do people presume (say, when they plan to get married) that their partner will die before their vows are exchanged in a public ceremony? Of course not!

When a baby is conceived, we presume *life*, not death. When you decided to become parents, your energy was focused on the *life* of the child you were bringing into the world.

People say of pregnancy that the mother is "expecting." Expecting what? Expecting that her child may not survive in the womb? Expecting that her child may die as an infant? No. The mother-to-be expects to give birth to a baby who is healthy, alive, full of potential, and deeply desired.

> The presumption is life—in the form of a baby the parents are preparing to cherish for as long as they live.

In a childbirth class, expectant mothers and their partners don't have long faces or talk of infant death. They have glowing, radiant faces and giddy, can't-hardly-wait-to-give-birth conversations with others in the class. The presumption is life—in the form of a baby the parents are preparing to cherish for as long as they live.

The death of your child is not how your story is supposed to end. But it did happen. And now you are left trying to make sense of this tragedy. It's so hard—hard on you, hard on your partner, and hard to make sense of. It's a devastating and unexpected blow.

If you feel as if you can't breathe or sleep or eat or plan or stop crying or get on with things, that's normal. You are grieving. That's how it is. Grief takes pretty much everything we have. It's all consuming, especially at the beginning.

Maybe you know why your baby died, or maybe you don't. There are way too many mysteries, and even if you do know, you surely wish it weren't so. We don't live in a culture where people expect babies to die. They do, of course. Now that you have experienced this, you will be alert to the stories of those who share your experience. But culturally, we don't talk about it, nor do we expect it. Our children bury us, not the other way around.

And now you are in the maelstrom of grief, finding it hard to function. This grief is so totally and thoroughly bewildering. Eventually, with time and intention, it will become less acute and overwhelming. For now, however, pay attention to your grief, and notice how it is affecting you.

We attended a support group soon after our daughter's death. We felt so shattered, and we found out that every other newly bereaved parent in the room did, too. We heard stories of not being able to get out of bed, of obsessing about the last time the parent saw the baby alive, of being unable to focus enough to pull dinner together, of experiencing nightmares or sleeplessness. Since then, in the course of our pastoral work, we have seen similar manifestations of grief, even when the story of loss was different from our experience with SIDS, such as stories of loss from miscarriage or a baby dying at birth. We have come to understand our own unconscious assumption that babies are durable and destined to live. Even though the threat of SIDS was there at the edges of our awareness, we expected both of our twin daughters to survive.

> If you feel as if you can't breathe or sleep or eat or plan or stop crying or get on with things, that's normal. You are grieving.

So we were staggered when one of our daughters died. How could this have happened? What if the feeling of being totally overwhelmed was our new baseline? How would we ever function like normal again?

## An Unexpected Blow: Trauma

When we get unexpected and devastating news that in an instant makes our once-familiar world feel strange and unknown, that's trauma. Psychologists use this label to describe the intense stress of a child's death and the constellation of symptoms experienced by the bereaved parent trying to live through it.

Physiologically, trauma has several consequences. When a child dies, stress hormones, adrenaline and cortisol, pour into the parent's bloodstream to prepare the body for "flight, fight, or freeze," the classic human stress responses. Instinct kicks in. The shock of the death affects the parent's heartbeat, breathing, and thought patterns. The experience of death scrambles everything at first. Some parents

### Thoughts about Self-Care

If you are feeling overwhelmed, we encourage you to stay with it. What you are experiencing is a normal part of grieving. Find a grief support group or a counselor who specializes in grief to help you believe that you will not feel like this forever, and get ideas for coping with grief.

- Local hospitals sometimes offer pregnancy and infant loss support groups. Call yours and find out.
- Search "Compassionate Friends" in your web browser, and find support in your area. The Compassionate Friends is an international organization that supports parents who are grieving the death of a child of any age.
- Talk to your pastor for immediate support and to find out about local options for help.
- Search "grief counselor" in your web browser or seek resources (names of counselors or organizations that might have lists) from your health plan administrator or your employer's human resources department.
- Call your city hall to ask whether your community sponsors any grief groups. Many communities offer these. If you can, find one that supports families whose young children have died.
- Ask to talk to a chaplain or social worker at your hospital. Some hospitals offer support groups for specific causes of death; at ours, we found a group for families who had lost babies to SIDS.

may be unable to function (freeze), some may actively reject the news and messenger (fight), and some may set emotion aside and either start strategizing or go numb (flight). Everyone seems to default to one of these stress reactions by nature. These reactions are the body's biological way of responding to a major threat.

For additional common symptoms of grief, see The Compassionate Friends website (https://tinyurl.com/ycbs9lt5). You'll find a list of symptoms there.

Thinking about the death of a child as a threat might seem odd, but it is a threat. All the hopes and dreams for this baby in your life have had an impact on you, even if you barely knew of the pregnancy. Each situation is different, of course, but suddenly facing the loss of what you thought was going to be true about your life is a threat to the future you imagined.

The news of this death upends the story you have been telling yourself about this new little one and your future as a parent. Your life is rewritten in an instant and completely out of your control. This trauma reduces your brain's ability to process what happened, making it especially challenging to cope, adjust, and come to terms with your baby's death.

So it's no wonder grieving parents ask, "How can this be happening?" In the midst of the shock of this experience of death, what we long for is not actually the *answer* to this question, though that would be good. What we need is *equilibrium*—a sense of knowing what's going on, of trusting that all will be well. In the acute phase of trauma and grief, equilibrium is in short supply. If you feel as if everything is being rearranged, that's because it is.

What is so disorienting to all of us who have experienced the death of a child is that we don't know how the story of life is going to turn out. The new story about life in the days ahead is being "written" while we live it. In fact, this has always been true, but now it's frightfully clear. We suddenly know that life is very, very precarious.

The new story about life in the days ahead is being "written" while we live it.

Each of us reacts to trauma differently. You and your partner will likely grieve differently, at a different pace, and have different grief triggers. This will be especially true early on, before experience teaches you what you might expect of the other. Unfortunately, this will be happening at precisely the time when you most need the other to be supportive. Remember that neither one of you has any spare energy or grace or gratitude. This is survival mode, and it can be tough.

We immediately discovered that we would grieve differently, and it was evident at the moment we discovered our daughter's lifeless body in her crib. Catherine moved into planning mode: stop our surviving twin's crying by nursing her, call 911, call the grandparents to let them know. David was nearly immobilized by the shock. He knew something horrible had happened, but he could not move to action without direction. Can you see "flight" and "freeze" at work? Neither reaction was wrong. It was what our bodies did in response to the shocking reality we were just discovering.

As you can imagine, however, in the intensity of that moment, Catherine felt impatient that David couldn't think, and David felt rushed into responses he wasn't ready to make. We had to learn over time to give each other space to grieve. Thankfully, that first moment of discovery was the time when our differences were the most poignant and counterproductive in relation to the needs of the other.

## Another Kind of Loss

For some parents, the physical loss of a baby seems to put at risk another kind of loss—their identity as a parent. For the pregnant woman, identity as "a mother" can become a powerful reality from the moment she knows she has conceived (and maybe even earlier, while trying to get pregnant). For her partner, it may take a bit longer to feel like a parent. But once a child is conceived, the expectation of childbirth gathers momentum, and the identity of "parent" becomes a fact of life for mothers and their partners. This process is much the same for adoptive parents. Once you start on the path to parenthood, you start to feel like a parent.

Remember what you did to get ready? If you lost your baby early, maybe you were just starting to prepare. If you lost your baby later, maybe you had already pulled together a nursery. You painted and decorated and furnished it, all joyful tasks. You made decisions about color(s), toys, books, and bedding. Perhaps you chose a crib. And of course, there were the diapers, the onesies, the sleepers, not to mention a stroller and a car seat. Selecting and acquiring these are first steps in preparing for and imagining oneself as a "parent."

So when does one become a parent? For biological parents, is it only after the birth of a live, healthy child? Or does it happen when the child in the womb is viable or at conception? Do adoptive parents take on the role only after the child moves in? We think you become a parent as soon as you commit to being a parent, and that might be well before birth or adoption. Likewise, your status as a parent does not change because your child died. You will not get to raise this child, but you are no less a parent.

And how old does a child have to be for parents to feel grief when that child dies? Does it happen when a child is three months old? With a stillbirth at 38 weeks? As early as a few weeks of gestational age? Before the adopted child comes home? Such examples involve children who were imagined into being and almost always deeply desired and already deeply loved. Once you are a parent, you will grieve the loss of a child, no matter how old the child was or how much time you had together.

You love this baby. That's why it's so hard. This intensity is all about love—and loss.

We spoke with a woman in her midthirties who had just gotten married, and she and her husband started trying to conceive right away. Joyfully, she was pregnant within a couple of months. They were thrilled. Then, at the three-month prenatal visit, the ultrasound revealed serious problems with the fetus. The condition was life-threatening not only for the fetus, but also for the mother. She was devastated, as was her husband. They needed to make a difficult decision about whether to continue the pregnancy. When this baby died, she wondered, would they still be parents? Yes, oh yes. A nonparent would not have struggled with this decision. Though they would not be able to raise this child, they were absolutely parents.

Clearly seeing herself as a mother and parent helped her turn to her grief more completely. She did not spend her precious energy avoiding her baby's death by wrestling with an intellectual question about her maternal identity. Instead, she could think about how she would mark the passing of this child and grieve feely with her partner and others who love her.

## The New, Unwelcome Story

Some parents lose babies early in pregnancy, some late, some at birth, and some soon after. Some hear the news of an impending death before the baby actually dies, and for some, the death itself is shockingly sudden. There are so many versions of the story of loss, each with its own unique story line, but all of our stories share this fact: we did not expect our babies to die. Because our babies died, our lives got flipped upside down. Our lives have a new and unwelcome twist now.

When you announced your pregnancy or told people you had received news of a baby from the adoption agency, you no doubt heard plenty of affirmation and congratulations. People get excited about new babies. Babies are amazing, joyful, and hopeful, even from a distance. Once the baby arrives, announcements abound, and people can't seem to get enough of the details. How long were you in labor, or how long did you wait for the baby from the time you

> Expect that *every* fetal or infant death will be devastating for the parents.

---

Caregiver Tip

*Don't* imagine that parents will feel less traumatized or will see it as a kind of "blessing" that their baby died early in the pregnancy. Some caregivers imagine that the pain is less because (they reason) the parent has had less time to feel attached. This is simply not true! Therefore, expect that *every* fetal or infant death will be devastating for the parents. This assumption will never let you (or them) down.

heard that the birth mother chose you? How much does the baby weigh? What color eyes? Hair? When can we come to visit?

No amount of oohing and aahing seems to be too much when it comes to the celebration of a new baby. However, stories of infant loss are hard to tell, because they run counter to the joyful stories of children who are healthy and alive. Who is eager to hear a sad story?

Here's an important thing. Your new, unwelcome story is the one you are discovering now. Though others may not always be able to hear your story, you must be able to tell it, especially to yourself.

## Frozen-in-Time Moments

When a child dies, you feel as if you've suddenly been transported to an alien world—one where the rules about life, death, parenting, plans, and future are all twisted out of shape. There are likely images and sounds, smells and feelings that vividly keep coming back to you.

David recalls riding in the ambulance to the hospital after we called 911 and the paramedics came (as is protocol when a child dies unexpectedly at home). He looked out at people walking as if nothing had happened. By their expressions, they appeared to be still living in the same world they had inhabited when they awoke. He, however, was riding in an ambulance with the body of our eight-week-old firstborn daughter. This was not the same world we had inhabited just a few hours earlier.

Catherine remembers the moment the paramedics appeared in the nursery—specifically, the look on their faces as they surveyed the picture before them. She was in the rocking chair, nursing our surviving twin to calm her. David was standing by Erin's cold body on the changing table, already tuned into the fact that she had died without us near. Our sweet dog was hovering, trying to make sense of all the emotion she was picking up. The paramedics looked so confused for that first moment—as confused as we were. Nothing made sense to any of us. Then their training took over, and they started doing what they were taught to do: check vitals, perform CPR, and transfer the body to the ambulance.

All of our stories share this fact: we did not expect our babies to die.

Your new, unwelcome story is the one you are discovering now. Though others may not always be able to hear your story, you must be able to tell it, especially to yourself.

Every parent of a child who has died carries with them moments that are "frozen in time," as if all the details are seared into their memory. This is not unlike some of our nation's traumas. The bombing of Pearl Harbor (December 7, 1941) is described as "a day that will live in infamy." One moment, it was a fine December day. The next, it was fire and sinking ships and chaos. And on September 11, 2001 (9/11), people went to work in the World Trade Center's twin towers in New York. Before the day was out, airplanes flew right into the buildings, thousands in the towers died, and the buildings had collapsed into dust that chased terrified New Yorkers who had survived. School shootings and astonishing natural disasters (tornados and tsunamis), when observed or experienced in person, are events that survivors carry for the rest of their lives.

Think about the day you got the news of your child's death, even if it's hard. It may have begun with what was expected to be a routine visit to the prenatal clinic. You recall that the technician doing the ultrasound was having trouble finding the heartbeat. "I think I need some help," the tech said. "I'll be right back." You may recall thinking that maybe the ultrasound machine was acting up—certainly just routine stuff. Then the doctor came in. You will never forget what the doctor said to you: "I'm so sorry. Your baby has died." It's the sucker punch you did not expect and could not believe was coming true.

Or, maybe you recall the day when your normally active baby stopped moving in the womb. A growing instinctual fear led you to call your doctor and then go in for a visit. You remember hearing the same unforgettable words: "I'm so sorry. Your baby has died." Even armed with this instinctual fear, you were not prepared to hear these words or believe that your baby was dead.

We encourage you to call up your memories, even if they are very painful. Take the time to let them sink in. Think about what your senses experienced and what you felt emotionally. Write down these feelings if that helps, or gather up mementos that embody these early moments. Therapists who specialize in trauma sometimes talk about *metabolizing* the trauma by reviewing it, feeling the pain, and observing how it affects you. The more you avoid and deny the pain of the loss, the less healthy your healing will be. It will be hard to get the memories out of your head anyway. They will come unbidden. Allow yourself to cry and be sad. By doing so, you help yourself move beyond shock. You start making this new story yours.

Allow yourself to cry and be sad. By doing so, you help yourself move beyond shock.

## Thoughts about Self-Care

Concretely gather your memories. You may not keep them forever, but for now, they will help you process your loss.

For example, if a clinic visit was where you heard the news about your baby's death, these are some ideas to help you remember and process it:

- Do you have a note with the appointment place and time written on it? Keep that.
- Did you get a written summary from the clinic visit? Keep it for now.
- Jot down what you remember:

  — What was the day like?
  — What prompted the visit?
  — What time of day?
  — Were you cold as you waited?
  — Who delivered the news?
  — What did you say, if you could say anything?
  — How did you decide what to do next?
  — Who did you consult or call?
  — What did you feel? Anything other than shock?
  — What happened next?

If you didn't learn the news at a clinic visit, for your situation, imagine how you could gather up reminders, either in concrete things, like paper or baby clothes, or in recorded memories similar to the list.

## In Search of a Reason

If you can't get that frozen-in-time moment out of your head, that's your body trying to make sense of it. Or if you can barely remember those moments, ironically, it's the same. When you have experienced something as traumatic as your child's death and feel so unmoored, it is reasonable and normal to try to make sense of what has happened, and this can lead to difficult questions about the cause of your baby's death. Whether your questions revolve around your own behavior or your partner's during the pregnancy, or your caregiving after birth, your mind and heart will make an effort to know what contributed to your baby's death.

Many women who carried the baby will focus on their biological responsibility out of instinctive and fierce parental love. Any of us could make a list of common questions: Should I have done something differently? Was it the glass of wine I had? Was it my diet—what I ate or didn't eat? Was it my lack of exercise, or too much exercise? The antibiotics I took before I knew I was pregnant? The stresses or worry I never managed to leave behind?

The fact that mothers ask these questions so frequently and ponder them so thoroughly reveals the depth of their love. What other kind of love would take on this painful self-reflection, which asks, By having changed my behavior, could I have changed the outcome and prevented this death?

It's normal for partners who were not carrying the child to tap into their own archetypal role as parent as well. They, too, know the baby was completely dependent. They have the responsibility to protect the baby's life and provide for their well-being. This instinct runs deep and strong—so strong that, when a baby dies, partners too can feel as if they have failed to protect their child from death.

For most of us, there are no easy answers. Miscarriage is almost always a mystery, and it's rarely consoling to say that there must have been something wrong with the fetus that made its death reasonable and merciful. The causes for stillbirth and early infant death are no less mysterious.

Some of us do know we could have done better, but isn't that always the case? And isn't it true that some babies survive even in the most difficult of circumstances?

You can torture yourself about this and likely will. It can take a long time before you feel as if your baby's death was not your fault or before these kinds of questions aren't front and center anymore. After all, it was your child who died. It happened on your watch.

This sense of responsibility and failure is hard to shake for another reason. Ironically, if you imagine that a change in your behavior might have prevented your baby's death, you can also imagine that you might somehow be able to ensure that it never happens again with another child, a spouse, a friend, a pet, or anything or anyone who is dear to you.

## Being Vulnerable

The truth is, death is capricious. There is no guarantee that any of us will live through this day. One feature of the trauma of pregnancy and infant loss is that we can't ignore this truth the way we can when we are not in the midst of a loss. Every day is precious, as is every life. In the midst of the daily grind, we can come to take this for granted, especially about those who are closest to us.

In addition, you may find that your child's death sparks grief for other losses you have experienced, on top of this one. You may find that you are suddenly hyper-aware of the well-being of other people you love. When the capriciousness of death is glaring, it can take up an inordinate share of your internal life. It's exhausting.

## The truth is, death is capricious.

In addition, you may find that your anxious hovering over others is unwelcome. Consider the impact of the following behaviors:

- Overreacting to the late arrival of a spouse whose errands took longer than you expected
- Being hypervigilant about the whereabouts of surviving children
- Taking a rigid stance on nutrition that might not fit the rest of the family.

But why shouldn't you be keenly attuned to life's fragile nature? You have just experienced intimately the fragility of life and the closeness of death, so statistics and platitudes are empty data. Anyone can go at any time. Psychologists talk about the possibility of grieving parents even experiencing symptoms of post-traumatic stress disorder (PTSD), something more often discussed as an affliction among veterans of war.

Within a year of our daughter's death, we took our surviving twin in for a well-baby check. Our nurse spoke glowingly of how well she was doing. In her conversation, the nurse joyfully leaned into the future, wondering what our daughter might choose as a vocation when she grew up. When the nurse left the room to retrieve something, we looked at each other and talked briefly about how confident she seemed about our daughter's survival. We validated between us that we took nothing for granted and acknowledged that we were wary about looking ahead in hope.

The nurse returned and continued to care for us and our daughter. Before the visit was over, the nurse revealed that some years previously, she had lost a three-year-old to a freak ear infection. We were stunned. She seemed so happy! Her gift to us was this glimpse of what it might be like to be open to the future again, even after such a profound loss.

Experiencing the death of a child makes us terribly vulnerable to the ways in which our culture denies death. Many of our parents and grandparents lost children through miscarriage and never spoke of those children again. It was not culturally encouraged. So much of the advertising we see every day is focused on how to stay young or at least look young. The old and infirm are not present in media, and death is rarely mentioned unless it's sensationalized by scandal or tragedy. Even though children are vulnerable, dependent, and yes, mortal beings, we tend to focus on seeing them as innocent, cute, playful, curious—full of life in all its potential.

Though our elders might not have spoken much about the children they lost, most did not forget them. After our daughter died, we were surprised by how many older people came to us as their pastors to tell stories of children's deaths, especially stories about miscarriages, stillbirths, and early deaths. We were inspired by their courage and heartened for ourselves that they had not forgotten these children, even many decades after the children had died.

We more easily view the very old as "nearing death" or at the "end of life." We do not view children this way. While not wrong, this attitude can and often does get in the way of accepting that children die, too. Though every adult and child is mortal, it feels true to say that we parents wish that our love might be powerful enough to keep our children from facing death. This fierce, protective love mimics the love God displays for God's own mortal children.

In Old Testament Israel, when King David's young-adult son Absalom died, David grieved powerfully: "O my son Absalom, my son, my son Absalom! Would I had died instead of you, O Absalom, my son, my son!" (2 Samuel 18:33b). The story of his death, a murder, is complicated by war and kingdom politics, but regardless of cause, David experienced the death of his child. You can read the whole story in 2 Samuel 18 and the first part of chapter 19.

As time goes on, your grief will no longer run your life, as it does in the beginning, but it will never go away.

Though so difficult, the pain you feel is directly proportional to the love you have for your child. You would not be grieving if you did not love. Your love for your child is a profound vulnerability, and the grief will accompany you for the rest of your life. It is a testament to that love. You will not forget the child you lost. As time goes on, your grief will no longer run your life, as it does in the beginning, but it will never go away. You will always miss this child and the future with them that is not to be.

## For Caregivers

Every parent is taken off guard when their child dies. Most say, "We never saw this coming." And the death of a child always shakes a parent to the core. This loss is unlike any other.

The death of a child always shakes a parent to the core.

Family and friends almost always underestimate the devastation and disorientation parents experience when a child dies. This response, unfortunately, tends to make a horrible situation feel even worse.

When a child dies, parents ask, "How can this be happening?" *But they are not looking for reasons.* The question is rhetorical and expresses bewilderment, betrayal, and disbelief. When we hear this question, a better translation would be "I can't believe this is happening."

What parents really need in this moment is someone to sit with them in their bewilderment. They certainly don't need "answers." There aren't any.

Grieving parents don't need "answers." There aren't any.

Grieving parents need companionship—other people who can endure the silence, the emptiness, and the heartbreaking tears, all without giving advice or imagining there is a quick fix. But this kind of companionship is really hard to offer, because it demands a capacity for vulnerability and empathy in a culture that defaults to solutions and resolution.

What generally happens instead of quiet companionship is that family and friends try to say things that are positive and hopeful to help the bereaved feel better. This frequently takes the form of explanations or platitudes. "Everything happens for a reason" is a popular response. Another is "At least you're young and can try again to have another child."

As well intended as they are, these kinds of attempts at positivity are what people say when they don't know what to do with their own discomfort and awkwardness. These responses are intended to be caring. But they are actually a response to the speaker's fear that this cavernous grief will swallow them whole if they get too close to it.

So you begin to see the disconnect here. The grieving parent whose grief feels overwhelming can't receive comfort from the caring friend or family member who rushes to "help" *before* seeking to understand the nature and depth of the parent's grief.

### Sympathy versus Empathy

A lovely three-minute video by Brené Brown, research professor at the University of Houston, sheds light on this disconnect by contrasting sympathy and empathy.[1] Brown observes that sympathy tends to stand at a distance and offer platitudes. It does not take the time to listen to and understand a person's anguish and despair. Rather, it invents "at least" statements: "At least you're young and can have another child." "At least your baby died young, before you had time to get really attached to them."

So why don't grieving parents find this kind of response very helpful? In practice, people tend to offer sympathy when they want to stand at arms' length from the misfortune. They come close

> Brené Brown came to our attention through an excellent TEDx Talk she did on the power of vulnerability.[2] Her area of research is shame, and she has written several books, including *The Power of Vulnerability* and *The Gifts of Imperfection*. Whether she is speaking or writing, her down-to-earth language and accessible manner create a feeling of connection and safety that inspires learning and growth.

enough to utter words intended to be comforting but keep far enough away (emotionally) to avoid getting dragged down into the mire of the misfortune. Grieving parents feel the distance and know that nothing more can come from this encounter than a comforting word or phrase.

However, when a caregiver is willing to stop and stay, to listen deeply a            tions, such companioning involves a willingn            sk and vulnerability. Per Brené Brown, this is er            ort video, Brown depicts empathy as the respons            es down into a pit in order to sit alongside a persc            athy unhurriedly seeks to understand the gravit            f the situation. It demonstrates love and suppc            ith the person until a next step is taken.

An empathetic person understands that nothing can or will make this terrible situation feel better. Yet she or he stays with the bereaved so they might feel less alone. The goal is not to help them feel better, for what could make them feel better? The goal is that they feel less alone in their grief.

It's important to see the difference. Many people tend to offer sympathy because they are trying—usually in a short period of

The words of Psalm 139 call out God's empathy and accompaniment:

[O Lord,] Where can I go from your spirit?
    Or where can I flee from your presence?
If I ascend to heaven, you are there;
    if I make my bed in Sheol, you are there.
If I take the wings of the morning
    and settle at the farthest limits of the sea,
even there your hand shall lead me,
    and your right hand shall hold me fast.

(Psalm 139:7–10, NRSV)

time—to help the despairing person feel better. The instinct isn't bad, but sympathy does not provide real support, because it doesn't get to the magnitude of the loss.

The point here is to help caregivers understand what would be truly helpful to someone who feels as if they will never be happy again. To use the words of Brené Brown again, to be supportive, you need to be empathetic. You don't have the power to make things better. You do have the power to be a companion along the way.

Faced with the question in this chapter's title—How can this have happened?—we might be tempted to respond with platitudes and infant mortality statistics. But bereaved parents are facing a deep gulf between their love and commitment to their child on the one hand and, on the other, the child's absence from their life due to death. That gulf, that separation, is painful to the point of despair—at least initially and for a time.

To be supportive, you need to be empathetic.

Facing that gulf, parents say things like "I'll never be happy again" and "Life as I know it has ended" and "I could as well have died with my child." Naïve friends or family members, assuming they are also well meaning, at some level sense this gulf. But while they may see the gulf as foreign and unfamiliar, they too often imagine that there is a way over or around it. For this reason, their attempts to be caring often fall short of being understanding and supportive.

What bridge can span the gulf of "I wish I were the one who died, not my child"? What path would you recommend when a parent says, "Life as I know it has ended"? The deep gulf that separates parents from a child is not like a temporary road closure that can be easily managed by a detour. Know that the parents of children who have died must live with the relentlessness of their grief. It does not take days off—not for many months and sometimes years.

Though empathy is what they need, bereaved parents can feel selfish or put off seeking help because they don't want to expect others to muster the capacity, stamina, and courage to walk with them through the devastation of their grief. Caregivers who develop the capacity to provide this kind of support can give a treasured gift. It will not be forgotten.

## For Reflection and Discussion

### For Bereaved Parents

1 You are likely reading this book after the earliest days of your grief. What did you learn in those early days about your reaction to trauma? What physical symptoms did you notice? What do you still experience?

2 How are you remembering your child? What do you have and what have you done to help you remember your baby?

3 What comments have you heard from friends and family that have been especially helpful? Especially unhelpful?

4 Where have you found support outside of your family and friends? What has been especially helpful?

5 How have you noticed your grief changing over time?

### For Caregivers

1 When you first heard about the loss of this child, what went through your heart and mind?

2 You are likely grieving this child's loss, too. What have you done to support yourself in your own grieving?

3 Have you consciously set any structure around your caregiving? None of us has limitless time, but are you communicating once a week, once a day, every other week? What can the bereaved parents count on from you?

4 If you haven't already done so, are you able to help with meals, provide child care for surviving children, or simply offer your empathy? Could you ask others to join you in providing this kind of care?

# Resources

## *Articles*

### GRIEF AFTER PREGNANCY AND INFANT LOSS

Babbel, Suzanne. "Miscarriage and Post Traumatic Stress Disorder." *Psychology Today*, November 16, 2019, https://tinyurl.com/y92qdu6t.

> This article sheds light on PTSD related to miscarriage, but this idea also applies when a child is stillborn or dies following birth. Though the article focuses on mothers, PTSD can also affect fathers.

Compassionate Friends. "To the Newly Bereaved: You Are Not Alone." https://tinyurl.com/ycbs9lt5.

> This page on the organization's website offers an extensive list of symptoms of grief.

Davis, Deborah L. "Nine Compassionate Tips for Surviving the Loss of Your Baby." *Psychology Today*, October 24, 2016, https://tinyurl.com/yb9hylz6.

> Dr. Davis offers helpful ideas for grieving, coping, and adjusting to the death of your child. Dr. Davis also wrote *Empty Cradle, Broken Heart: Surviving the Death of Your Baby* (Golden, CO: Fulcrum, 2016).

Gillihan, Seth J. "21 Common Reactions to Trauma." *Psychology Today*, September 7, 2016.

> Working with PTSD, Gillihan proposes that one trauma can take on many faces.

Mayo Clinic Staff. "Infant Death: Grief and the Path to Remembrance." Mayo Clinic website, March 17, 2018, https://tinyurl.com/yaettzxf.

> This article encourages us to find ways to provide solace in our grief so we can move toward finding joy in life again.

BBC News. "Miscarriage can trigger post-traumatic stress disorder." November 2, 2016, https://tinyurl.com/y8bxckvy.

> This report features a personal story about the impact of multiple miscarriages.

Leis-Newman, Elizabeth. "Miscarriage and Loss." *Monitor on Psychology* 43, no. 6 (June 2012): 56, available at https://tinyurl.com/yckgpzm2.

> This article reports research that counters the cultural notion that miscarriage is not a significant loss. The impact on fathers also is discussed.

## Books

Erickson Barrett, Elise. *What Was Lost: A Christian Journey through Miscarriage.* Louisville: Westminster John Knox, 2010.

> Drawing on her own experiences and interviews with others, Pastor Erickson Barrett brings a theologian's sensitivities to this topic.

Horchler, Joani Nelson. *SIDS and Infant Death Survival Guide.* 3rd ed. Cheverly, MD: SIDS Educational Services, 2003.

> This is a broad-ranging look at loss from SIDS and other similar causes of death.

Ilse, Sherokee. *Empty Arms: Coping with Miscarriage, Stillbirth and Infant Death.* 21st ed. Tucson, AZ: Wintergreen, 2017.

> This book is particularly good in guiding newly bereaved parents as they navigate the decisions and questions that arise immediately and in the days and years to come. It also offers an excellent bibliography and resource section. It has been updated regularly since it was first published in 1982.

# 2

## Why Do I Feel Like This?

PERHAPS THE funeral is over or you have returned home after a D&C procedure following a miscarriage. The cultural and medical activities that mark the death of your baby have run their course. For most of your friends and family, your child's death will begin to fade into the background. You will get a few days off work for medical or bereavement leave and then face the cultural expectation that you will tidy up your grief and get back to normal.

We are here to tell you that grief will be your companion for much, much longer than a week or even a month, and you will never get *back* to normal. Those who specialize in working with people in grief often say we need about three years to become who we will be as a result of the death being grieved. Maybe a three-year timeline is good news to you because you are relieved to know you will not always feel the way you do now. Or maybe that seems like an agonizingly long time to live in grief. However that timeline feels to you today, we want to assure you that, while the old normal is gone, you *will* find a new normal in time.

You didn't get to take a class on surviving grief. You are living your life in the midst of it, creating your new normal every day from now on. In this chapter, you'll learn more about grief, how it may affect you and your relationships in the days and years ahead, and what choices you have about your grief path.

## The Landscape of Grief

Grief is more than the feeling of sadness. In fact, you may find that a dizzying array of feelings begin to surface. Sadness, of course. Numbness, emptiness, and confusion, too. But you'll also experience distraction, weariness, anger, indifference, impatience, irritability, sensitivity and insensitivity, exhaustion, fear—the list goes on, until your world is flooded with feelings.

When we aren't in grief, emotions tend to be more predictable and familiar. Grief, however, tends to open the floodgates, and the strength and unpredictability of feelings that come up can be unnerving. We can start to wonder if our emotions will ever calm down. Let's look at some of the emotions of grief that can be most distressing.

### Confusion

Why did this happen? How could this have happened? Should this have happened? What reason(s) might there be for such a thing happening? These questions press for some kind of response, even as we sense there are no easy answers and possibly no answers at all. Still, these questions call to us. Why?

We need to know, or at least try to understand, what happened to our previously well-behaved and generally predictable universe. As we mentioned in chapter 1, our grief can make the world suddenly feel alien to us. In the world we thought we knew, babies outlive their parents. In this new world, tragically, that is not always the case. Grief drives us to revise our understanding of the world to include tragedies such as ours. Our confusion is the sign that learning to feel at home in such a world will take time.

As this slow adjustment is occurring, we cannot help but wonder, "What else is going to go wrong?" We once assumed that when we wanted to drive to work, our car would start; and when we used an appliance, it would work; and when we turned on the shower, the water would be hot. Yet when a baby dies, it can feel as if we can't

*You will never get back to normal.*

take *anything* for granted. Why wouldn't the car and refrigerator and dog all die, too?

It's not uncommon for us to feel as if a once friendly, kind, and trustworthy world has suddenly turned on us. Are we being punished? Is the punishment fair? Is there any way to "get on the good side" of the universe again? Is it crazy to think this way?

The people of Israel (as depicted in the Old Testament) also felt confused at how the world could feel so nurturing one moment and so cruel the next. First they were a chosen people; then, with the rule of a new pharaoh, they became slaves in Egypt. They wandered forty years in the wilderness, then found refuge and home in a "land of milk and honey." They enjoyed a stable government under the rule of kings David and Solomon, then saw their kingdom overthrown, and they were carried off as exiles by conquering empires. How did the people of Israel learn to trust God despite their experience of suffering and death? This is a central theme of the Old Testament.

Whether we consider their confusion about the benevolence of the world or our own, it is no easy matter to rebuild trust that the world (or even God) is not out to get us. We'll talk about this more in

In a timeless example from the Bible, Job has lost his children, plus his possessions and health. In his grief, he imagines that it would have been better not to be born than to have to endure all this suffering:

"Why did I not die at birth,
    come forth from the womb and expire?
Why were there knees to receive me,
    or breasts for me to suck?
Now I would be lying down and quiet;
    I would be asleep; then I would be at rest."

(Job 3:11–13)

the next chapters, but here it's enough to say that when we cannot understand how the world works, this confusion can be unsettling and even exhausting. It is unsettling because we don't know what we can count on. And it is exhausting because if we feel we live in a world that is at best ambivalent toward us, we end up being constantly on alert, waiting for the next tragedy to strike.

## Fear, Anxiety, and Vulnerability

In the weeks and months after Erin died, we lived with an anxiety we had never known before. The coroner was very careful to say in the autopsy report that nothing had apparently been wrong with our daughter, that she had clearly been well cared for, and that we could not have anticipated or prevented her death. But this was not comforting for us as we considered the life of our surviving daughter. Catherine, especially—given that she was breastfeeding and therefore had so much close physical contact with Cara—began to feel rising panic even when nursing that Cara would die in her arms. Even more distressing, she feared that Cara would die when we weren't near. We have pictures of Catherine sleeping as Cara slept on her belly. We felt compelled to be with her all the time.

We had been advised to use an apnea monitor on Cara after Erin's death. (Such a monitor is worn around the rib cage, and an alarm sounds if it doesn't detect breathing.) After several false alarms, we decided to move her into our bed, so if the alarm went off, we could tell immediately whether she was OK. We had so many alarms in that first month that Cara was admitted to the hospital for observation. It was an enormous relief to know that others were also watching over her. The hospital recalibrated the monitor over a couple of nights, and we had far fewer alarms after we went home. This helped, but she slept between us until she was two years old.

Not long after this, Catherine realized the panic attacks were intensifying. She sought out a grief counselor, who helped her realize that this loss was indeed a trauma, and her unconscious desire to save our surviving daughter from death was, frankly, not possible. Rather than constantly focusing on the idea that Cara might die, she learned to direct her thoughts toward her love for Cara. It took time for Catherine to make this shift, but the strategy was helpful. This reframing was equally valuable when our subsequent daughter was born a few years later, and even when our grandson was an infant thirty years after that.

Not everyone will have a surviving infant to take care of in the midst of fresh grief for another baby. However, the stark reality of the precariousness of life, seeing how quickly life can be shattered, is ample fuel for anxiety and fears of all kinds. It can revisit years later in other precarious situations.

Prior to the death of your child, you might have walked across a dark parking lot without thinking of getting mugged. Or you might have assumed your partner would remain healthy for decades, unlike a neighbor just diagnosed with stage 4 ovarian cancer.

There are countless fears we usually have safely corralled in pens labeled with signs like "Unlikely to happen to me," "Not to worry," and "This can be avoided if you're careful." But grief can cause us to make up new signs for the pens where these fears reside: "Unlikely doesn't mean it won't happen," "There's good reason to worry," and "Being careful is no guarantee of anything." The imagined protective barrier between ourselves and illness or misfortune feels as if it's precariously thin. We feel anything but protected or safe.

In some areas of life—say, at home—doors can be locked to ensure safety. But what keeps illness and death at bay? No door or lock can do that. While this has always been the case, grief makes our lack of control suddenly and unavoidably obvious. The new normal of grief does not assume bad things won't happen (again) to us or our loved ones. That time of innocence is gone. Rather, grief teaches us to live in the full knowledge of this reality—that everything that can happen to people could also happen to us.

For a time, you will likely err on the side of caution as you live into this new reality. You might choose to avoid driving when the roads are icy and snow covered. You might pay attention to warning signs of illness, rather than ignore them as "probably nothing." The stable of behaviors you consider high risk has probably grown. You know all too well that no one is invincible. And though it may seem burdensome to know this, this awareness can also help you live with greater appreciation for any time that is *not* marked by illness or misfortune. Furthermore, it can inspire you to live with greater intention.

"There's always tomorrow" is something people think or say when death hasn't visited them unexpectedly. *You* know that today is the only day we can count on, as the Psalmist said: "This is the day that the Lord has made; let us rejoice and be glad in it" (Psalm 118:24). If we look at vulnerability as a coin with two sides, we could label one side fear and the other side *carpe diem* (Latin for "seize the day"). This flip side of vulnerability prompts us to say to ourselves, "Don't wait. If it's important, do it now. Tell people you love them today. Cherish life today."

No one likes feeling vulnerable. But this feeling drives the recognition that we are mortal beings. We can get sick. We will die someday. The non-fear-based side of vulnerability invites us to live with awareness of our limitations and finitude *and* inspires us to make the most of every moment we are alive. Mindfulness practices are designed to help people live fully in the present moment. Grief, ironically, can help us do the same. And that is a gift.

### Loneliness

The worst thing you could imagine happened when your child died. But despite this worst-case scenario, the world does not come rushing to your doorstep with an abundance of empathy. Rather,

> This is the day that the Lord has made; let us rejoice and be glad in it.

Google "mindfulness," and you'll find a wealth of information. Mindfulness is essentially any practice (meditation is a common one) that helps you focus your attention on the present moment (versus ruminating on the past or worrying about the future). Jon Kabat-Zinn is credited by many for reintroducing this ancient practice to Western medicine.[1]

family and friends often keep their distance, possibly due to their own fear and uncertainty about what to do or say. This can leave you feeling quite alone. Some even say they feel abandoned.

It's possible that Jesus felt like this when praying in the Garden of Gethsemane as he faced his imminent betrayal, trial, and death. He wanted and needed his disciples' support, so he said to them, "I am deeply grieved, even to death; remain here, and stay awake with me" (Matt 26:38). But while he was praying, the disciples fell asleep. Since their support was so important, Jesus asked them a second time to stay awake, and also a third time. Yet each time, they fell asleep. The disciples were unable to recognize the importance of the moment. They could not see Jesus's sorrow and grief. They noticed their own feelings of weariness, but not Jesus's grief and loneliness.

When your grief and sorrow are invisible (or barely visible) to family and friends, and when it's very visible but they don't know what to do, it is easy to feel alone. In response, your loneliness may propel you toward self-care. It can push you to seek out support groups. It can invite you to take bubble baths, light candles, and listen to soothing music. More negatively, loneliness can also foster isolation and withdrawal. It can cause you to view others with disappointment and to feel resentment, judgment, or anger. It can cause you to turn inward and take on an array of unhealthy behaviors like overeating or not eating at all, sleeping too much or not enough, or using alcohol or drugs to numb emotional pain. It's likely you will experience both positive and negative inclinations as you grieve. Recognizing this can help you to forgive yourself for impulses that are less charitable and to affirm yourself when your choices are kind and nurturing.

Finally, when thinking about your loneliness, try not to view it simply as a problem to be solved by companionship or self-care. Your loneliness is also a sign that your child's death *has* set you apart from most of the people you know. Loneliness reminds you that what you are really lonely for is your child. You long to hold your child again and love them. This aspect of loneliness you will always

Bible scholars label some of the Psalms as "lament" psalms. Most lament psalms describe our loneliness in the midst of suffering. For example, Psalm 22 (usually read at the end of the Maundy Thursday service during Lent) begins this way:

My God, my God, why have you forsaken me?
    Why are you so far from helping me, from the words of my
      groaning?
O my God, I cry by day, but you do not answer;
    and by night, but find no rest.

Though the psalm eventually turns to words of hope (verse 24), it realistically depicts the agonizing time of waiting for this hope to appear.

carry with you—eventually not so much as a burden but as a lasting testimony to your child's preciousness and your love. So let this aspect of loneliness persist, and learn to call it by name—the name of your child.

A member of the congregation we were serving at the time, the mother of one of the kids in the youth group, came and sat with Catherine sometimes when David was in evening meetings after he went back to work following the twins' births. Powerfully, she continued to do so

## Tips for Caregivers

How might caregivers respond to the grieving parents' loneliness? Here are some ideas:

1 Communicate: call or email or text. Ask the parents how they are doing, and cultivate the trust it takes to support them by giving them the time to really talk. Ask questions, probe, and let the tears flow without jumping in to fix it. Bring tissues—good, soft, comforting tissues.

2 Bring them food, and ask if they want company. If they do, offer to stay and eat with them. Again, listen.

3 Invite them someplace where unexpected tears won't be a big deal. Maybe it's your house for dinner, a long walk, or watching TV together.

after Erin died. This was a thoughtful antidote to the loneliness that Catherine felt when David was away. The level of work to be done was less—just one baby needed to be fed and changed and soothed, not two—but her presence was such a gift.

## Exhaustion

It's common for grieving parents to have little energy to do anything. At times, you might not even want to get out of bed. Starting anything new is almost impossible. The exhaustion of grief is more than being physically tired. It's a weariness compounded by wondering, "Now that my baby has died, is anything worth doing anymore?"

Normally, we assign meaning and purpose to the things we do. For example, we might cook and clean as an expression of hospitality to others. Or we might exercise and bathe because we value taking care of our body. In grief, we can find ourselves thinking, "Why should I take care of my body? Who cares whether I cook or clean?" For a time, none of these things may feel truly important.

Early on, it may seem as if the only thing that is important is the death of your child. So that is where you'll be inclined to spend your time and energy, which means you may feel little motivation to spend your energy on anything else. Lacking energy and motivation for all the other aspects of life can leave you worrying whether you'll ever regain the energy and motivation you need to engage life's other demands. That worry is exhausting, too, and fosters a revolving door of weariness that is common to all who grieve.

This exhaustion doesn't simply disappear. Rather, it seems to linger until we regain the perspective that many aspects of life are still important. Our grief counselor once told Catherine that just getting out of bed each morning is a victory. From there, we take tiny steps toward engaging with other aspects of life.

At some point, you will decide anew how you want to spend your time and energy. Stop doing things you find depleting or that lack meaning. Devote yourself to that which you value and find inspiring. When you feel your energy returning, you'll see that grief has actually helped you see and focus on what is truly important.

In the months after our daughter's death, it occurred to David that she wouldn't want him to give up on life and would feel bad if he did (as if she were the cause). He realized then that his life going forward could be dedicated to her memory. He decided that he wanted his life to reflect the wonderful and profound difference she made. So David began to see her life and death as a catalyst for living with renewed purpose and imagination. At his best, David likes to think she's proud of the life he is now living. This is a happy outcome when compared with the exhausting first months of grief.

## Self-Assessment

"How am I doing?" This already difficult question is made more so when you ask it of yourself in the context of grief. If you want to be in control or are known for being an "Energizer bunny" or like yourself best when you are upbeat and outgoing, grief can really challenge your view of yourself. Even when grief is new and raw, you may still want others to think well of you or even admire you. It's common to be self-conscious about how you're doing, which comes with its own set of feelings.

In grief, you can be disappointed with yourself, too. You may also notice that you are being self-critical, impatient, and demanding: "Quit feeling sorry for yourself. Pull yourself together. Stop crying all the time. You can do better than this." Whatever the messages you hear from your inner critic, know that they are common, even expected. No one likes feeling and dealing with the ravages of grief for long. And if it occurs to you to try powering through it, well, that's a normal response. It rarely works, but many try.

In our seminary preparation to be pastors, our pastoral care classes taught us some lessons about grief, among them Elisabeth Kübler-Ross's proposed stages of grief: denial, anger, bargaining, depression, and acceptance. When our daughter died, we actually talked between ourselves about how this knowledge might trim our grief journey. That was not to be, although her invitation to think about grief at least invited us to seek some perspective about what we were experiencing. Grief had its way with us, and we slowly learned to let it follow its course.

Failing to power through grief isn't really a failure, though seeing that it isn't can take time. If others seem to be doing better with their grief than you feel you are doing with yours, that's an illusion. You are doing your best. Period! There's no comparison between your grief and another's grief, because each person and situation is unique. Again: there is no failure in grief. Once you see that, you can begin to treat the feelings of grief as teachers—showing you the paths of healing that are just right for you. (We'll say more about this near the end of this chapter.)

When Catherine first visited a grief counselor, she asked if Catherine was getting out of bed for her day. "Of course," Catherine replied. "I have a baby to feed." Then the counselor asked if she was taking a shower most days and eating food in the course of the day. "Well, yes," Catherine replied. "Are you able to talk to your husband?" asked the counselor. "Yes, of course, though I cry all the time." The counselor then looked right into Catherine's eyes and said, "Then you are doing very well."

"What do you mean?" Catherine asked. "That's barely getting by. I'm a mess."

"Yes, you might be, but you could also just be sitting in a corner, not functioning at all. You are doing much more than that. You are caring for yourself and your baby, and you are staying in touch with your

Though Kübler-Ross's work helped break the social taboo of talking about death and dying that existed in her day, there is no subsequent research to support stages of grief. For some, this model became too prescriptive and thus unhelpful. As we discovered, grief is not something that ends or resolves. It changes, yes, but it is a life-long companion that will not be hurried or prescribed.

husband. That is actually quite good." This was a powerful moment of grace, and validation of the enormous challenge we were facing after the death of our daughter.

## Sometimes…Humor

Few would disagree with the statement "Grief is no laughing matter." But what if something strikes you as funny? Is it OK to laugh? Will others think well of you if you do? Is it appropriate? At the funeral for our daughter, her surviving twin had a big noisy poop. The loud sound and juxtaposition of this very human function against the quiet, otherworldly feel of the funeral service evoked subdued laughter from us. Our smiles at this potty humor likely helped us release pent-up tension and, ironically, stay more alert to all that was happening in that moment.

It can feel odd, and wrong, to laugh when grief has been so intense and front of mind for so long, but experiencing joy again will be good for your soul. Be curious about an instinct to laugh or an awareness that something is funny. In many ways, this signals a small amount of healing, a clue that the intensity of your grief will not last forever.

## Needing Respite

Asking "what if?" or pondering "If only" represents the yearning to turn back the clock, to have a life other than the one you are now living. You may feel the desire to somehow leave this mortal existence, with all its rough roads and battering storms, and find refuge in an Oz-like land—somewhere over the rainbow, where happy little bluebirds fly. These flights of fantasy are not found just in movie scripts. Many people in grief spend bits or even chunks of time daydreaming of such a refuge.

It's hard to say whether this habit should be encouraged or not. Spending endless time dreaming of some way out of your grief is obviously counterproductive, because this kind of fantasizing is actually a distraction from the work of grieving. But what about

It can feel odd, and wrong, to laugh when grief has been so intense and front of mind for so long, but experiencing joy again will be good for your soul.

doing this on occasion, when the burden of grief seems too great to bear? In the world of medicine, when a person is terminally ill and suffering terrible pain, there is an intervention called "palliative sedation." Medications induce a (brief) coma-like state so that the suffering person has a temporary respite from the pain. Some daydreaming can function like this. In any case, it's hard to criticize anyone for wishing for a place of tranquility and beauty. So be gentle with yourself when you take a fantasy break. Just name it for what it is, and then let it go.

Given the vast scope of grief, it's no wonder that it is accompanied by a similarly vast set of feelings—profound, intense, and often unfamiliar to us. Mewlana Jalaluddin Rumi, a thirteenth-century Sufi mystic, provides great advice for those who grieve. In his poem "The Guest House," Rumi imagines that feelings of all kinds come knocking at our life's door, and he speculates that we'd rather keep some of them out. So he writes:[2]

> Welcome and entertain them all!
> . . . . . . . . . . . . . . . . . . . . . .
> because each has been sent
> as a guide from beyond.

Rumi invites us to trust that despite the harshness of the death(s) we grieve, there is an energy in the universe (some call this God) working in us and for us. We are invited to consider that each of the many feelings grief inspires is a seed of healing and renewal. This doesn't make the grief feel less overwhelming, but it does draw us to consider that the devastation of grief can and does lead to the fruitfulness of grief. Where once there was nothing, now a seed germinates. And we can wonder, "What will this seed become if I tend to it?"

### Humility

Sometimes grief reveals to you less flattering beliefs or habits that are important to realize, even if you don't feel ready for this revelation. For example, maybe you have been critical of others who "go on too long" in feeling sorry for themselves. Now, in your grief, you may have gained more insight into the way time and grief actually work themselves out. Grief has revealed your judgment to you and will invite you to choose whether this judgment is one you want to keep.

Grief may reveal a belief that sounds something like this: "When it really counts, people need to get it right!" If you notice that you feel self-righteous when someone says something unhelpful to you in response to your child's death, and if anger comes quickly when someone misses the mark, that might be a clue that you are demanding perfection of others—and likely of yourself as well.

Grief can make us impatient, but there is grace to make mistakes and to learn. Grief can also make room for forgiveness and patience and education. You can learn to forgive yourself for your clumsy attempts to be helpful in the past *and* forgive those whose attempts to help you were clumsy.

Grief doesn't demand that you change anything, but it often leads to change, because it can give you eyes to see what is important and what is not. Given a chance, grief will inspire you to live with as much grace as possible, because deep inside, you know grace is what you desperately need, as well as what others likely need, too.

Through these discoveries, we learn humility. Everyone starts life as an imperfect human being. Grief reminds us (reveals to us) that this condition does not fundamentally change as we age. Yes, we may become wiser and more mature, but never perfect. Humility allows us to see and accept this reality. Humility is also at the heart of faith. Humility reminds us that God and others love us as we are, even and especially in the midst of our imperfections.

## First Steps toward Healing

In the first chapter, we spoke of the difficulty of integrating this new event, your child's death, into your life story. It's not one you want to have to add, and you know it will affect everything from now on. How will you tell your life story now, to yourself and to others? We also mentioned the challenge of telling this story to others who may not have the skills to hear it with empathy. Especially once we get past the cultural markers of death, like funerals, grieving parents are kind of adrift in a world that may or may not know about their loss.

However, telling your story—to yourself and to others—is an important contributor to your healing. It reinforces your memory of the precious few days you had with your child, whether your child was in utero or in your arms after birth. It also requires you to interpret the story in some way and make meaning of it. This interpretation is also integration—making the story your own—and is especially healing. It is part of the work of grieving.

Remembering is the first step. What happened? What did you feel? What happened next? Writing, touching, and holding "artifacts," speaking your child's name, hearing it from someone else, hearing about another person's experience of those early days (a grandparent or neighbor, for example)—all of these actions help you remember. You will likely cry or be on the verge of crying when you do this remembering. Let the tears flow, even if you feel like they will never stop. Remember, these tears are your love for your child.

Grief doesn't demand that you change anything, but it often leads to change, because it can give you eyes to see what is important and what is not.

## Self-Censoring

Remembering is vital to your move toward a new normal, but you really can't do this alone. Your story and its meaning will be shaped by those to whom you tell it. However, grieving parents are often keenly aware that talking about their child's death might not always be welcome.

When you see pregnant women, when you attend baby showers, or when you are with couples showing off their newborns, you surely feel some internal instinct or pressure to keep your story to yourself. You may feel that to "insert your grief" into the happiness of others' lives is selfish or insensitive. You may imagine that these other parents have a right to insulate themselves from your grief, as if it might be contagious. You may even think that to share your story can cause nongrieving parents to feel doubt and fear that they otherwise would have kept at a distance.

And what if it's a big holiday where the official mood is happiness and celebration? What would happen if you told your stories then? You might imagine others saying or thinking, "Why do you have to ruin everybody's day with your sadness?"

When we refer to "artifacts," we mean concrete things that carry or prompt memory. Here are some possible examples:

- A piece of clothing your child wore, like a sleeper or the hat worn home from the hospital
- A blanket or toy from the crib
- An item you purchased in anticipation of your child's birth, such as a piece of clothing, décor for the nursery, or a car seat, even if it never got used
- A medical report
- Cards from loved ones about your loss
- Pictures of your family, your baby, or you (thankfully, it's becoming more common to take a family picture when there has been a stillbirth or a baby dies soon after birth)
- A copy of the funeral bulletin or obituary

You may feel that to "insert your grief" into the happiness of others' lives is selfish or insensitive.

Real or imagined, these thoughts are hard to get out of our heads. The sadness you feel is so vast that you cannot help but wonder where it belongs. And judging from the vibe or the very real and unwelcome responses you get from others, you might feel like your sadness doesn't belong anywhere. It needs to stay inside you.

Meanwhile, as you witness nongrieving parents being asked constantly about their pregnancy and their newborns, you notice your own deep yearning for people to ask you about your child, too. Know that it is natural, normal, healthy, and vitally important that you are able to talk about your child.

But this puts you in a bind. You *want* to tell your story. You *need* to tell your story. Yet you worry that there is no good time to tell it and no situation where your story belongs.

Even now, three decades later, we are conscious of this dynamic. When someone asks us, "How many children do you have?" we always have to ask inside whether the person asking the question is ready to hear the whole story. Often, when it's just small talk, we say, "We got to raise two daughters." That is true. We didn't get to raise our first. But we know it's not the whole story, and with that knowledge comes a tinge of grief, even now, so many years later.

### Finding a Safe Place

So where *does* your story belong?

You *want* to tell your story. You *need* to tell your story. Yet you worry that there is no good time to tell it and no situation where your story belongs.

For starters, your story could belong in a pregnancy and newborn loss support group. You will know your story belongs there by the looks you get (often with tears) when you arrive. And you will know your story belongs when you hear the other parents share their own stories of grief.

In a helpful support group, mothers talk about their pregnancies—how they were going, what they were feeling. Parents talk about clinic visits and normal worries as the weeks ticked by. And they share details about their babies, including what it felt like to hold them after they had died.

In a helpful support group, others listen intently and empathetically. No one seems impatient. No one responds with explanations. You will see and feel a deep sense of caring. Tears flow freely. Your story is at home among these others who know your grief as well as anyone could, because they have been there. Just to gather with these other parents and sit in silence would be enough to feel supported. Yet stories *are* told, because everyone present wants and needs to hear.

We knew the safety, support, and love of such a group. For us it was a SIDS (sudden infant death syndrome) support group for newly bereaved parents. We attended this group just five days after the death of our daughter and continued going for months.

Over time, it becomes easier to put into words what you need to say about your child's death. But initially, you may notice that while telling your grief story is important, it is also confusing. It is confusing because the "self" who is telling this story is in the process of being remade.

You may find yourself starting to tell your story, then suddenly quitting and saying, "I don't know why I said that," or, "I never used to cry, but now I can't stop crying whenever I talk about it." It's as if you don't quite recognize yourself as you are talking. The fact that this is a normal part of grief is little consolation at the time.

Feeling self-conscious when telling your story also is to be expected. When telling your grief story, it's hard not to notice the utter silence and rapt attention others give you (in the right settings). It can feel as if you are onstage. And if you can't quite find the right words to tell the story of your child and your grief, it can feel embarrassing.

There is no remedy for this other than to keep telling your story. In time, you will learn that however you give voice to your story is good enough. You'll become acquainted with your vulnerability and will learn to be gentle with yourself when your words seem inadequate. And you'll come to trust that others will somehow always hear in your story the great love you feel for your child who has died—which is the essence of what your story is trying to convey in the first place.

## Navigating Grief as a Couple

If you are partnered, you and your partner might want to be telling the same story. You hold a lot of it in common. But . . .

It would be nice if couples always walked hand in hand in grief. It would be nice if, say, when one parent was sad or angry, the other was calm and strong to receive those feelings. But as you have already learned, it is common to feel out of sync in grief.

You may choose to write a poem about your experience, while your partner seeks a time of wordless silence. You may want to visit the cemetery, while your partner wants to go to a movie. Going to church, being sexual together, being with friends, starting house projects—any of these moments can give rise to an experience of "we're really in different places right now."

Before your grief, you might have been confident that you could work out these differences easily. In your grief, you may not feel so sure. Grief can temporarily rob you of patience and leave you feeling less charitable toward others, including your partner. When this is the case, mounting the energy to work through these moments of disconnection (real or perceived) is hard. While this kind of friction is common in grief, it is also unsettling. You don't want to lose your partner, too! Talk about a double tragedy.

Partnered couples necessarily want to walk hand in hand through life's ups and downs. Psalm 23 (RSV) speaks to this yearning in these words: "Yea, though I walk through the valley of the shadow of death, thou art with me." To trust that God will walk hand in hand with you through the valley of the shadow of death can be comforting. Walking hand in hand with your partner is surely comforting, too. But when you feel as if you are walking solo, what then? Will the friction stay? Will your paths continue to diverge? Will you ever come together again?

With all of the uncertainty, unfamiliarity, and strong feelings, it's no wonder that what arises in grief can seem like a flood that threatens to sweep our very lives away. We encourage couples to stick with it. Seek help from professionals if you need a safe place to negotiate your grief together. Many couples report that the work they invest in these difficult days pays dividends over a lifetime. You share a devastating experience, and you can survive, even eventually thrive, together.

In the next chapter, we'll talk about how we keep our heads above water. But it has been important to describe the terrain of grief with enough detail for you to be convinced that this is not a stroll in the park. When you feel overwhelmed, you need to know why this is. It's not a failing on your part! You are facing one of the most complicated, bewildering, frustrating, gut-wrenching, and mysterious experiences humans can encounter in the course of their lives.

## For Caregivers

If you are a caregiver, thank you for reading along and working to become more understanding of the grief process and how to support grieving parents.

Let's begin with "the new normal" for grieving parents. Some life events are like a detour when driving—they temporarily force you to alter your course, but soon you're back on familiar roads and heading toward your desired destination. Grief feels more like a natural disaster that has destroyed your home. Grieving uproots and relocates. You can't go back to your home. It's gone.

Try to imagine how you might feel if you were suddenly uprooted from a familiar life and relocated to a place where things feel strange and unfamiliar. Words like *unsettling* and *dislocated* are metaphorically and literally accurate descriptions of grief. What can you, as a caregiver, say about this that's helpful to grieving parents?

Simply asking, "How are you doing?" is less helpful and may even sound insensitive to a person in grief. This is a polite greeting in our culture, used in everyday encounters. For someone devastated by grief, it's too much of a shortcut. Thus, it's more helpful to say, "What has the past week been like for you?" or, "What are you noticing or feeling today?" These latter questions allow room for people to speak about their grief and don't imply that you only want a short reply, such as "Fine." To use the language of empathetic communication, try to ask open-ended questions that invite thoughtful and honest reflection.

Asking open-ended questions is an exercise in imagination and humility. David recalls participating in a Co-Active Coaching exercise.[3] He was directed to ask open-ended questions one after another, and the person receiving his questions was directed to rate their impact. David was surprised that some of the questions he liked best were given only a so-so rating, while some of the questions he thought were only so-so received a strong rating. This taught him to let the person receiving his questions determine their impact and choose which of them to engage.

Caregiver Tip

Closed questions are those that have a simple, predictable, and known answer: How old are you? Where did you grow up? What is your job? These are polite questions that generally feel safe to ask and are easy to answer.

Open-ended questions invite reflection and don't have predictable answers. These kinds of questions have the potential to produce insight and promote a feeling of connection. Here are some examples:

- How does it feel to be your age?
- What was it like growing up where you did?
- What do you like most and what do you like least about your job?
- What did you remember today about your baby?
- Tell me about how your grief is changing over time. What do you notice?

Ask open-ended questions as much as possible. Scatter them like seeds. And then see what they produce. Know, too, that sometimes your best questions may not produce an immediate response, because the grieving parent needs or wants to ponder them for a while. This is fine, even great. Their reply, whenever it comes, will be worth waiting for.

How about engaging a grieving parent who is feeling unsafe, vulnerable, confused, and/or fearful? Open-ended questions work here, too. And try to practice taking this perspective: be curious, not judgmental.

Be curious,
not judgmental.

Surprisingly, if a grieving parent tells you they are feeling unsafe, it might be unhelpful to offer reassurance: "You live in a safe neighborhood. Your house has an alarm system. You have a dog that hears and barks at everything." The problem is that this is a judgmental response. The rush to judgment assumes you know why this person is feeling unsafe and further assumes you know what to do about it.

In contrast, here is a curious response: "Tell me more about why you feel unsafe." These words assume you do not know why the parent is feeling unsafe. Ask questions, and listen until you come to a greater understanding. And then, if you have an instinct to help solve a problem, go at it this way: "Is there anything you can think of that might help you feel safer?" Retain this posture of curiosity (and practice it with others, too).

What if you hear a grieving parent express self-criticism? What if you hear them say something like "I should be doing better than this"? Again, get curious. Ask, "Why do you say that?"

Adopting curiosity may seem easy, but it gets more complicated when you agree with what the person has said. For example, what if they say to you, "I think I'm letting my grief run my life"? You may agree with them. Then what? Our advice is to resist the urge to tell them what you are thinking. Remember, you're practicing curiosity, not judgment. A curious alternative might be "What makes you think that your grief is running your life?" This will help them further explore their thought. It could be that they haven't fully accepted that their grief follows them everywhere. This realization, in turn, might even help them treat their grief as a welcome visitor (as in Rumi's poem "The Guest House," quoted earlier in the chapter). This perspective will be more helpful for them than thinking they are failing to keep their grief at bay.

What about the use of humor? Let's keep this one simple. If they initiate it, join in. If they don't, it's best to avoid it.

If you notice they seem exhausted, you could ask, "Would a distraction be helpful?" Then offer some ideas: bowling, a walk, a movie. Even though grief follows grieving parents everywhere they go, some activities do provide a bit of a respite. And if these ideas don't garner any response, you could also wonder with them if rest is needed. Grieving parents occasionally will choose not to care for themselves—almost as if to demonstrate the extent of their grief's devastation. A gentle "I'm concerned about you" is a caring response when you think this is the case.

Now, here's the flip side to "grief's devastation." Grief can also be verdant. It can inspire physical, emotional, and spiritual renewal. Grief can call forth personal growth that produces, in time, a life more abundant than the preceding one (which was not acquainted with grief). Rabbi Harold Kushner, in *When Bad Things Happen to Good People,* speaks eloquently to this point. He describes in detail the ways grief has enriched his life but then says he would gladly trade away all of these riches to have his son back again.[4]

This is the paradox. While grief can be grounds for growth, grieving parents would always choose to have their children alive instead. So celebrate personal growth whenever the grieving parent speaks of it to you. And remember that this growth comes at a great cost. It is always bittersweet. Be aware of your own desire to see your friend move into happier days. Sometimes the day is just sad. Stay with it.

When Rabbi Harold Kushner's son Aaron was only three years old, the boy was diagnosed with a degenerative disease that would mean death in his early teens. Harold wrote his best-selling book, *When Bad Things Happen to Good People*, to help himself make sense of this painful reality. First published in 1981, his book continues to inspire people who are living with tragedy.

How about a few more tips? Just kidding. You've had enough for now. So this is a good time to remind you that being a caregiver isn't about memorizing or practicing all this advice. We're trying to help you feel more competent and confident in supporting friends, family, or colleagues experiencing the death of a child. But at some point, it can feel like "Aiieeee, I won't ever remember all of this!" Then don't. Pick one caregiver tip from this section, and work with that. For example, practice asking open-ended questions, and for now don't worry about the other tips.

Grieving parents will generally be grateful for anyone who makes an effort to connect with them. Remember, it's not about being perfect caregivers. If the grieving parents can feel clumsy with their grief, you can feel clumsy with your caregiving. It's not a sin to be clumsy—even when dealing with something as important as grief. Daring to fail in an attempt to be supportive is brave and loving. Give yourself tons of credit for this. You deserve it.

## For Reflection and Discussion

### *For Bereaved Parents*

1 How would you describe the "normal" features of your life before this death? How is this "normal" changing? At this point in your grief, what do you make of these changes?

2 Prior to this grief, what feelings were most prevalent and familiar in your daily life? What less familiar feelings are now a regular part of your life? How comfortable are you with them?

3 How does the world appear to you now? What is your attitude toward learning more about this seemingly new world?

4 Imagine you are listening to the story of your child's death. What details of the story seem especially important? What details seem to be missing? What details would you deem too private to share?

5 What do you yearn to be true about your life? What does this suggest about next steps to take in tending to your grief?

## *For Caregivers*

1 What experiences may have prepared you to be a caregiver? What gifts do you possess for this work of love and support?

2 As you learn more about another's grief, what changes has this invited you to make or consider making in your life?

3 What about your world of feelings? Are you discovering something new about your emotional life as you interact with your grieving friend?

4 How would you tell the story of your friend's loss? What details about this story seem especially important?

## Resources

### *Articles*

March of Dimes. "Dealing with Grief after the Death of Your Baby." October 2017, https://tinyurl.com/yaflwdyv.

> This web page offers a condensed yet remarkably thorough, practical, and helpful look at how to understand and cope with grief after the death of a baby. This site also lists grief support groups and resources.

Muthler, Sarah. "Surviving Loss as a Couple." Seleni Institute, https://tinyurl.com/yd3m5763.

The author describes how grief stresses a partnered relationship and offers suggestions for keeping that relationship healthy and enduring.

## Books

Kushner, Harold. *When Bad Things Happen to Good People.* Anniversary ed. New York: Schocken, 2001.

Kushner writes from the experience of his son's illness and death. He seeks a way to honor the depth of human suffering, still believe in a loving God, and imagine how grieving can yet be life affirming.

Nelson, Tim, and Sherokee Ilse. *Couple Communication after a Baby Dies: Differing Perspectives.* Oro Valley, AZ: Wintergreen, 2008.

Bereaved parents Tim and Sherokee share wisdom gained from navigating grief as couples.

# 3

## How Do I Keep Going?

THE INTENSE feelings and overall upheaval of grief are so unsettling that they can make you wonder whether you can still navigate the challenges of your life. Furthermore, whatever coping skills you have previously developed are likely not quite enough to restore your confidence. Building on your coping skills will be a major theme of this chapter. But even before considering this confidence-building task, you will need to find enough hope to fuel your effort.

### Finding Hope

When hope is missing, it's hard to trust that anything good will come out of your grief. Without hope, you may also wonder what good will come out of anything you do. Nothing feels important anymore. Lethargy is common when hope is lacking.

Catherine felt this lethargy during much of the first year after our daughter's death. She had just gone back to school part-time, and she had the primary day-to-day parenting responsibilities for our surviving daughter after David went back to work. We were still new in our congregation, and she found it hard to be "public" in the way that might have been expected of the pastor's wife. She stopped sitting in the front and moved to a pew in the back of the church, which allowed her to slip out without lots of small talk. Most Sundays, she wore the same bedraggled outfit; she just didn't have the energy to work up to "Sunday best." Thankfully, if anyone disapproved, they kept their complaints to themselves. With time, energy for "going public" started to return. Eventually, she felt less avoidant about interacting with parishioners and found she cared more about what she wore.

The antidote for ambivalence is hope:

- Hope that the exhaustion, loneliness, confusion, and fear will eventually relent
- Hope that in time you will learn to bear this grief more as a companion than as a burden
- Hope that you can and will find the support and encouragement you need

Hope springs from many sources, but it can also feel elusive and hard to locate. Sometimes it will surprise you—like a gift you didn't expect in that moment. Other times, it's the product of much searching. So let's consider how hope shows up in the process of grieving.

### Hope from Ritual

For some of us, a ritual or funeral service may have marked the life and death of our children. Funerals or memorial services have traditionally been a way people acknowledge a loss and celebrate a life. We gather together to remind ourselves that humans throughout the ages have found a way to survive the ravages of death and loss. For those who did not have a formal, public ritual, the passing of a child may have been marked more informally. For either formal or informal rituals, including others is an important way to share the story of loss and grief, particularly when grief's weight feels too heavy to bear alone. Rituals can be a place where grief is acknowledged and shared.

Rituals allow us to speak about our hopes for the child who has died and about a future for survivors without him or her. In a Christian funeral or memorial service, for example, we confess ourselves to be in the presence of God, we offer prayer for those who grieve, and we formally commit the child who died to God for eternity. If the baby was baptized, we trust the baptismal welcome into God's family. If the baby was not baptized, we trust that God's

Humans throughout the ages have found a way to survive the ravages of death and loss.

creating and loving embrace holds them even in death. Hope springs from this trust in God's eternal love.

We scheduled our daughter's funeral service to take place five days after her death. The church was crowded. So many people came to try to make sense of this sudden and shocking death. People from our own congregation came, of course, and family. So did seminary classmates and professors, a group of midwives from the practice we had used, and our own friends and friends of our parents. We were comforted that our daughter's death didn't make sense to them either.

Ritual moves grief outside of ourselves. Ritual speaks a word of truth into the shock and numbness that dominate the world of those in early grief. The public acknowledgment of the baby's death is important and establishes the finality of this loss, spiritually and emotionally. This doesn't mean the grief is over, but ritual may help those grieving take a step forward, however small, toward life without this precious little one.

## Hope from Words

We feel fortunate that the words spoken to and for us at Erin's funeral were so memorably consoling—especially the sermon offered by a friend and teacher, the Rev. Sheldon Tostengard, based

> But now thus says the Lord,
>     he who created you, O Jacob,
>     he who formed you, O Israel:
> Do not fear, for I have redeemed you;
>     I have called you by name, you are mine.
> When you pass through the waters, I will be with you;
>     and through the rivers, they shall not overwhelm you;
> when you walk through the fire you shall not be burned,
>     and the flame shall not consume you.
> For I am the Lord your God,
>     the Holy One of Israel, your Savior.
>
> —Isaiah 43:1-3a

on the text we had chosen from Isaiah 43. His words honored our loss and also connected us to people who had faced death through the ages. He was gracious enough to share a written copy of his sermon with us, and we treasure it. Here is a portion:[1]

No sooner did God begin the mighty delivery of Israel than Israel found herself crossing the great water. No serene lake did she face, but the deep and turbulent waters of death. That water for Israel was the potion of breathlessness, the womb of Leviathan, the impossible obstacle to freedom and life. God had to intervene to part those waters. Soon, Israel stood shivering on the far, safe shore.

Don't you wonder why little Erin had to face that dark river so soon? Certainly David and Catherine must wonder that. Before she could talk, before she could walk, she came to the edge of that dark, rushing river which even the strong, the mature cannot ford. Little Erin could not swim those deadly waters but slid beneath them swiftly, easily, without a struggle. Some part of faith must wonder why. . . .

We like to think that babies are tough, and so they are. But they are helpless too, and fragile. Death can never be very far away. . . . Can there be any question that such a death reminds us that the great, dark river is just there, in front of us? That great river which might pull the ground from beneath our feet at any moment?

But don't you know, dearly beloved, that some days ago, at baptism, little Erin went down into that dark river with Jesus. Down upon her head the water came, once and again and again. It was the water that greens the earth and slakes our thirst, but it was also the water of every tearing cataract or water that calmly closes over the tired swimmer's head.

Down and down and down on her the water came, the water of life but also the dark water of death. She went down into those waters, that little one, and came safe to the other side, borne there in the arms of Jesus. She is asleep in Jesus' arms now and he knows her name, knows it well. And one day, when the trumpet shall sound, that name, Erin, will echo above all the great waters. . . . And on that day little Erin, who now sleeps in the arms of Jesus, will rise to shine like the stars and the sun.

For us, then and now, Sheldon's words powerfully capture our feeling of helpless terror at the image of our daughter slipping beneath the dark waters of death. His words speak to our greatest fear: that our daughter died alone, apart from our love. And they offer the great reassurance that our little Erin will never be forgotten. We almost always cry, even now, when we read these words.

The hope we felt at Erin's funeral was just a glimmer. It was not (yet) bright enough to banish the darkness of our grief. But even a glimmer of hope is important when you are grieving. Seeing the light at the end of the tunnel holds a promise of hope to those who feel as if the darkness will never end.

Where do you see this kind of light shining, if only dimly, in your life?

Grief is often portrayed as dark and foreboding, but in his poem "The Tenth Elegy," Rainer Maria Rilke speaks of "fields of blossoming grief . . . [and] herds of sorrow, grazing [there]."[2] This is surprising, because we usually associate the word *blossoming* with springtime and usually think of grief as a barren, leafless tree in winter. Rilke surprises by having us imagine grief like a tree that is *greening*. And his phrase "the herds of sorrow, grazing" evokes a picture of sorrowing people gathered together, grazing. We wonder: what are they grazing on? What is the "food" that renews their energy? And what strength and hope come from this communal grazing?

When grief is portrayed as blossoming, it suggests that the wonder of springtime is somehow at work even when grief feels wintry. When we are portrayed as grazing, we trust that we will find food for this journey. Some form of hope is embedded in each of these images.

Hunt for stories and poems that speak to you—that give expression to your helplessness, speak to your fear, and honor your remembering. Collect these in a notebook or folder. Read them

> Even a glimmer of hope is important when you are grieving.

frequently. Notice how and why they touch you. Let them renew your hope even as they acknowledge your deep suffering. And know that the consoling words you seek don't have to come from a book of faith or from a famous poet. In fact, many grieving parents find it helpful to use their own words and images to tell the story of their grief. We encourage you to do whatever provides the nurture and inspires the hope you are seeking.

Catherine's sister, Mary, who was serving in the Peace Corps in the mountains of Papua New Guinea, wrote these words after learning of the death of this niece whom she had just learned had been born. Her words were deeply consoling to us. Mary wrote,

> I called out softly, hoping that Erin—this child of light—might come to me that I might hold her just once. After a time she did come, lightly, on the leaves. She was as beautiful as I imagined she was. I looked up and turned my head to see her all around me. And then she held me. And when I was comforted, quieted, she reminded me of creation—how masterfully it was made. She told me of its perfection—the circle, its simplicity and its complexity—paradoxes. She spoke of the beautiful rhythms wherein each of us has our place. The forest soothed me and the stream lifted me again and I smiled and even laughed a little. I realized that Erin had left me, but left me with the forest and the stream and the wind—and was herself all of these things.[3]

These words were about our daughter, but maybe you can imagine your own child being spoken of here. Sometimes too, the words of others will inspire you to come up with words of your own, whether in the form of a poem or story. Share what you've written with others if you wish. The primary benefit will be to you. The effort of trying to put into words what you are experiencing requires reflection and observation. This is an effective way to start trying to name and tell what is true about you and your grief.

still
the damp stillness
waits for you
my little one
so long gone
and yet so short.
time has lost meaning
the pain lasts
and lasts
I cannot
breathe in
enough
to fill that
terrible empty space
that should be
your life
little one
I cannot breathe
for you.

—Catherine Malotky, written
about five months after Erin's
death

## Hope from Artistic Expression

For some of us, music may best express the dissonance of grief, and for others, movement or dance will. Perhaps art—drawing or painting or sculpture—captures best what you are experiencing and thus reflects back to you a sense of perspective, a distance that can help you frame and reframe your grief and your hope. Your creativity can be a reminder that, despite the death you are grieving, something inside you remains very much alive.

Remember that reconnecting with hope is mostly about cultivating your awareness that hope is present Keep your eyes and ears open to signs of life. Know that sometimes it's in your deepest grief that hope shines as the smallest of lights in the center.

When hope is elusive and it feels just too hard to find it yourself, then what's needed is the trust that it will somehow find you. Hope, of course, can visit you in the form of a friend whose unshakable confidence in and support of you inspires you to hang in there. Hope can also show up when you observe someone with a significant disability who is yet living with courage and passion. In this observing, you might be inspired to think that somewhere inside of you is a similar kind of courage. This can be a hopeful thought.

Hope can visit us when we are observing nature, too. Jesus tells his disciples to "consider" the birds of the air and the lilies of the field (Matthew 6:26–30). Like us, these birds and flowers face times of storm and drought, and yet, Jesus points out, look at how God cares for them. One way we might see God's care is in the way it inspires

Music has rich resources for helping us express our grief. Here are a few pieces we found moving:

- Philip Aaberg, "Earth Abides," on *Winter Solstice III* (Windham Hill, 1990)
- Johann Sebastian Bach, Violin Concerto no. 2 in E Major, second movement, Adagio
- Samuel Barber, Adagio for Strings
- Jean-Philippe Rameau, "Entrée de Polymnie" from *Les Boréades*

the carefree industry of the birds and the breathtaking beauty of the flowers. Observing (or contemplating) nature this way is a form of prayer, and it can be a source of hope when it reminds us of God's creative and loving care for us and for all things.

## Coping Skills

At birth, you were gifted with one remarkable and powerful coping skill. You could cry. You likely cried out the moment you were born and practiced it oh so often thereafter. When you were cold, you cried. When you needed clean diapers, you cried. When you were hungry or had an upset stomach, you cried. When you were lonely and wanted to be held, you cried. And since crying always worked, you did it again and again—until one day, it didn't work so well.

Once you learned to talk, your parents likely told you, whenever you were crying, "Use your words." They expected you to tell them what you needed and not leave them to guess. From this moment on, you began to develop other coping skills in response to the new difficulties you had to face.

Do you have early memories of this learning process? Maybe you once fell off your bike and skinned your knee when no one was around. So you practiced doing some first aid and self-soothing until a parent or friend appeared. Or maybe you once had a crush on a classmate who didn't give you the time of day. Possibly you cried (it's still helpful to do this, even as we age), wrote in your diary, and listened to sad songs about the heartache of love. Or maybe you didn't get a job you really wanted. You somehow convinced yourself that this wasn't the end of the world, maybe by talking to a friend who'd had a similar experience.

The coping skills you have are the result of this history. They represent all of the challenges you have faced in your lifetime and all of the responses you have made to those challenges. Some of the coping skills you possess are likely very effective, and others not so much. You can enrich or build on the coping skills you already possess to help you through this time of grief.

## Choose Your Perspective

Choosing the lens (perspective) through which you look at your life is one very important coping skill. You want a lens that helps you see things clearly and accurately, not one that distorts and clouds what you are looking at. You may have heard the phrase "He is looking at life through rose-colored glasses." This is a reminder that people do not all look at life through the same lens.

If we labeled these lenses, we might call one of them the "lens of comparison." This lens will focus your attention on whether you are better off than this person or worse off than that person. Another lens we might label "the lens of undeserved suffering." This lens focuses your attention on the untimeliness and unfairness of the suffering in your life. Here's a short list of other common perspectives through which you may look at life:

- If it isn't broken, don't fix it.
- Life demands our best effort; anything less is not good enough.
- There are winners and losers in life.
- Conflict is always bad; keeping the peace is always good.
- People get what they deserve.
- It's not good to make others feel uncomfortable.
- The world is a hostile place.
- There isn't enough (love, wealth, food) to go around.
- It's better to give than to receive.
- What you don't know can hurt you.

These are a few of the many lenses through which you could look at your life, though you may not even be aware that you are looking at things through a lens. However, once you become aware of this, you are able to assess whether a lens is serving you well or not.

And what makes any given lens a good one for you? A good lens employs all of your senses and wisdom and instincts in order to help you see the details and the whole of your life clearly and accurately. Or to use a metaphor, it allows you to see both the forest and trees.

You surely inherited—from family or friends or society—lenses that are now familiar to you. Finding another lens, another perspective, through which to look at life may require that you look through another person's lens (which is something like walking in another person's shoes). For example, Viktor Frankl's perspective might be valuable.

Viktor Frankl was an Austrian Jew who was swept up in the pogroms of the Third Reich. He was interned at Auschwitz from 1942 to 1945. There, Frankl endured the worst kind of suffering and brutality, aimed at convincing him that he deserved to die because he was less than human. Even in this dehumanizing context, Frankl held on to the perspective that how he chose to respond to his circumstances was the true measure of his humanity. No matter what was done to him, Frankl responded with actions consistent with his values, beliefs, and integrity. In this, he perceived himself being fully human in an inhumane environment.

Frankl understood he could do nothing to prevent his captors from killing him physically, but he vowed he would not let them crush his spirit. His books, written after the war, give witness that his spirit indeed survived—not just intact, but overflowing with a wisdom born of deep suffering.

Consider Frankl's perspective that being fully human is not a matter of what has happened to you, but of how you respond to what has happened to you. Your child has died. This is indeed a great tragedy,

> A good lens employs all of your senses and wisdom and instincts in order to help you see the details and the whole of your life clearly and accurately.

Viktor Frankl (born in 1905) was an Austrian psychiatrist and psychotherapist of Jewish faith who was imprisoned at Auschwitz (a Nazi concentration camp) during World War II, along with his pregnant wife, his parents, and his brother, all of whom died there. He survived his captivity and authored many books, the most famous being *Man's Search for Meaning* (Beacon, 2006). When that work was first published in 1946, Frankl titled it *Saying Yes to Life in Spite of Everything: A Psychologist Experiences the Concentration Camp*. It remains a powerful read.

maybe the greatest you will ever face in your lifetime. Few would blame you for sinking into complaint or envying others who seem more fortunate. Frankl himself did not blame those imprisoned at Auschwitz who chose this perspective. But his perspective does invite us to think of ourselves less as a victim of fate and more as the author of our life.

When you choose to see life as dishing out fortune or misfortune, you are likely to focus on whether you are getting what you deserve. This perspective robs you of agency—trust that the essence of your life grows out of your own beliefs and actions. Without a sense of agency, you feel powerless to do anything but beg or complain. And you are left to wonder, "Where do I direct my pleading or my complaint?" You feel like a victim.

When you choose to view life as an opportunity to decide how you will respond to your circumstances, you have agency. From this perspective, you know you always have the power to respond to whatever is happening to you in a manner consistent with your beliefs and values. This perspective keeps the focus on your choices and responses, instead of on what should or should not be happening to you.

This sense of agency allows you to live the life in front of you. It keeps in check your wish to be living some other life. Viktor Frankl surely didn't want to be at Auschwitz. But he spent his time there not wishing he was somewhere else but rather living as fully as he could.

> Being fully human is not a matter of what has happened to you, but of how you respond to what has happened to you.

## Thoughts about Self-Care

Practice adopting an attitude of agency. Think about a time recently when you felt victimized by a circumstance or another person. Consciously consider how you might rethink that time not as a victim but as someone with agency. Consider responses that reflect your values and beliefs. Which of these responses might have moderated your sense of being victimized? Notice how this response could have affirmed your sense of agency and helped you see yourself as fully human, with all that is unique (and good) about you.

## Choose Support over Self-Sufficiency

Receiving support remains important for a long time. You might feel as though you ought to be able to do your grieving work by yourself. Note these common cultural messages we receive:

- God never gives you more than you can bear.
- When the going gets tough, the tough get going.
- Pull yourself up by your bootstraps.

If you are already inclined toward self-sufficiency, you may be tempted to think that seeking support is an admission that you are failing to deal with your own problems as you should.

The upside of the desire to be self-sufficient is that you learn how much you can do on your own, which is generally quite a lot. In the process, however, you also learn what you can't do on your own—this at the expense of receiving support along the way when it's most needed. Therefore, a coping skill that you may want to develop is that of knowing how and when to ask for support.

How to ask for support? David quickly learned he was not good at this. He had a hard time just coming out and saying, "Are you willing to help me by [name of what he wanted]?" (for example, going for a walk, processing feelings, or talking about an impactful poem). His natural habit was to talk around what he needed and hope others might guess what it was. As you might expect, this was rarely successful.

Some people have a knack for knowing how to ask for support. They do it straightforwardly, with no apparent shame at either asking or having their request turned down. "Are you free to go for a walk with me today?" They make it sound so simple. If the reply is yes, they express gratitude. If the reply is no, they thank the other for their consideration.

Family rules, personal habits, and cultural messages can keep you from asking for support or at least can cause you to feel hesitant to do so. What's ironic here is the overly high value many people place on self-sufficiency. Once you have experienced caring support and

A coping skill that you may want to develop is that of knowing how and when to ask for support.

have learned how much others love and value you even when you need help, you will wonder why it took you so long to learn this lesson. So don't wait. Practice asking for help now and whenever you need it. You'll likely still err on the side of asking for less than you really need. Remember, though, that the road of grief is long and hard. Having support along the way makes this difficult journey easier to bear.

### Choose Self-Care

Practicing self-care requires that you know why you need to do it. We assume you want to live a rich and meaningful life. We assume you want to engage—with your best energy—your grief and everything and everyone that is important to you. And we assume you want to do this sustainably. This is the aim and purpose of self-care.

If you have taken the initiative to read this book, it's likely that your biggest obstacle to living in a sustainable manner is the failure to acknowledge your limits and to set boundaries around your time and energy. Even in grief, you will be tempted to live up to others' expectations of you (whether these are real or perceived). You will be tempted to make a list of the things you "should" get done every day, and then be critical of yourself when you fall short.

Self-care is the set of habits that allow us to live sustainably. Through self-care, we develop strategies and behaviors that allow us to maintain our stamina and well-being so that, day after day after day, we can fulfill responsibilities and use our gifts in service of others.

David sees a parallel between those he worked with in Alzheimer's caregivers' support groups and those who are grieving the death of a child. The support group participants were often very hard on themselves when they could not meet the growing needs of their failing spouse. The caregivers were uniformly remarkably good-

Some people are more comfortable acknowledging their needs and asking for help. However, if they give themselves over to helplessness, this is no better than being unable to ask for support at all. The art of self-care in grief is finding a healthy middle ground.

hearted, generous, and well intentioned. But they consistently failed to notice their own physical and emotional exhaustion. And why was this? It was because they were focused only on the work that had to get done. What they needed to do was notice and account for the fact that human energy is a finite resource. Giving 110 percent is not sustainable.

The driving belief motivating this behavior is "where there's a will, there's a way." Studies indicate, however, that willpower is not unlimited. Humans not only can, but often do, run out of resolve. You may have noticed, for example, that the more fatigued you are, the less willpower you seem to have.

You cannot simply power your way through grief. You need more than willpower alone. Even the best self-care habits won't help you meet every demand placed on you, especially when those demands exceed your capacity. Good self-care thus begins with an assessment of the finite energy you have available. Only after that assessment do you consider how you might respond to all the demands on your time and energy.

Do you already assess your energy and well-being? Most people would say no. So where to start? Physical tiredness may sound easy to assess, but often it's not. You might be used to simply powering through it, and that always worked—until this time of grief. Or, because of this grief, physical exhaustion may be such a constant companion that you barely notice how you are actually doing.

Even in your grief, with its frequent emotional ups and downs, you may be able to notice when you are more irritable, impatient, or judgmental than is normal for you. Even in grief, you can notice when you're mad at the world and don't want to give others the benefit of the doubt. Even in grief, you can notice when you are

> Notice and account for the fact that human energy is a finite resource. Giving 110 percent is not sustainable.

For more reading on willpower, check out *Is Willpower a Limited Resource?*, a report published by the American Psychological Association (https://tinyurl.com/ycgo4nx4). It lists other sources of information on the topic.

behaving badly (below your own standards) yet trying to justify it. These can be clues that you are depleted. You are running on empty.

There are other emotional clues as well, if you know where to look for them. For example, if you are generally easygoing and flexible, notice when you instead feel uptight and rigid. If you are generally charitable and forgiving, notice when you are critical and unwilling to forgive. If you are generally patient and calm, notice when you feel impatient and anxious.

The point of this self-care assessment is to notice whether you are being or acting like your usual self. This might sound a bit confusing after reading chapter 2 on feelings. You might be wondering, "How do I distinguish the mad and sad feelings of grief from the mad and sad feelings I have when I keep driving myself to do more? Is this even possible?"

Yes, it is possible. But it requires you to notice where these feeling come from. Sometimes you feel mad or sad because you want your child back. Close your eyes, and you'll see that your child is at the center of these feelings. But sometimes you feel mad or sad because you once again said yes to a demand even when everything inside of you screamed, "No!" In this case, when you close your eyes, you're likely to see a people-pleasing habit at the center of these feelings.

Being able to feel your feelings and know where they come from is a foundational element of self-care. This awareness and attention to

## Thoughts about Self-Care

Whenever you're asked to do something that may require substantial energy or time, try responding this way: "I'll think about it and get back to you." When you're alone, sit in some comfortable place, and take slow, relaxed breaths for one to two minutes. Then notice how the request makes you feel. If a voice inside you is announcing, "I can't imagine taking on anything more right now!" then you know you need to decline. But if your internal voice says, "This sounds appealing to me," *then* consider how much time and energy you have to commit. Offer that information about your limits along with your affirmative reply.

your emotional state allows you to notice your overall well-being or your lack of it. Your ability to notice when your baseline emotional state is off gives you an early-warning system, alerting you to stress or depletion. Being aware of whether your physical and emotional gas tank is empty or full gives you a way of engaging or limiting your activity accordingly.

What if you are *not* inclined to pay constant attention to your emotional state of being? Another option is to ask more concrete questions like these: "Can I keep going at this pace? Am I running my life, or does it feel like my life is running me? Do I want off of this treadmill?"

A hospital patient once shared this little rhyme with David:

> When in danger,
> or in doubt,
> run in circles,
> scream and shout.

They laughed together, but you could also reframe these words seriously. Are you running in circles? Do you often want to scream and shout? This may be a sign that you're running on empty.

The work of self-care requires experimentation to sort out what will replenish and renew your body, mind, and spirit. For example, perhaps you feel exhausted. Do you need more sleep or rest? Then give that a try. If more rest doesn't seem to help, try exercise. Still not feeling replenished? Maybe you need to spend time with a friend, seek inspiration from art or poetry, or meditate. Ponder what might be helpful, and then give it a try. You'll gradually get better at guessing what might help.

### Choose to Manage Stress

Grief is stressful, and we are biologically hardwired to respond to stress. This was an evolutionary advantage for our hunter-gatherer ancestors, but it can be more detrimental than helpful for

Being aware of whether your physical and emotional gas tank is empty or full gives you a way of engaging or limiting your activity accordingly.

The work of self-care requires experimentation to sort out what will replenish and renew your body, mind, and spirit.

us modern humans. The fight, flight, or freeze reaction to stress demands that we notice and respond to whatever is in front of us. In fact, biologically, stress diverts our decision-making capacity from thoughtful consideration to instinctive protective responses.

How can you know that stress is driving your responses? When stress kicks in, the stress hormones (adrenaline and cortisol) increase your blood pressure and heart rate. These might not be as easy to notice, but stress also produces a breath pattern that is rapid and shallow, which is easier to notice. Recall what happens to your breathing when you watch a horror movie or anything suspenseful; it's likely rapid and shallow. We can deliberately slow that breathing down. Let your breathing become even, deep, and relaxed, and the stress response dissipates, as if your body is thinking, "You wouldn't be breathing this way unless you felt safe."

Stress responses are always aimed at resolving an immediate threat, which is demonstrably helpful if the threat perceived is a house fire. In that situation, what's needed is only to rescue family members and flee to safety immediately. But when the "threat" is grief, reactive short-term responses are generally not helpful over time.

Stress prompts us to choose whatever will *immediately* help to resolve the distress we feel. When stress is constant, we may choose to medicate the pain through alcohol, drugs, gambling, eating, sex, shopping, and the like. These diversions can provide the quick fix that stress demands, but they are almost always detrimental in the long run, because *they are diversions* and distract us from the real work that needs to be done: grieving the loss of a child.

Our stress response isn't concerned with the long-term consequences of our actions, because it frankly believes that if we don't survive this moment, we'll be dead. Unfortunately, when we are stressed, we are rarely aware that this reactive logic is driving our actions. Because stress never looks beyond the current moment, it doesn't consider longer-term issues such as these:

- What is the natural consequence of eating all this ice cream?

> Our stress response isn't concerned with the long-term consequences of our actions, because it frankly believes that if we don't survive this moment, we'll be dead.

- What will happen when the credit-card bill arrives?
- What will happen if I keep calling the same person for support day after day?

The stress reaction could be seen as a tyrant who wants to micromanage your self-care practice. This is the reactive you, not you at your creative, thoughtful, strategic, calm, confident, and imaginative best.

Stress will always exist in our lives as long as there are things we care about that can be threatened in some form. Threats to our health, employment, relationships, financial well-being, and the like are all experienced as stress. Eliminating stress is impossible. Managing stress in healthy ways *is* possible. We can focus our energy on stress management. Stress is a clue that grief is hard.

> We can focus our energy on stress management. Stress is a clue that grief is hard.

### Choose Your Daily Routine

Humans are creatures of habit. That is, humans tend to repeatedly engage activities that are enjoyable, meaningful, and important. One upside to this habit is that life takes on a familiar shape and structure; it becomes routine. One downside is that we can begin to engage these activities without much conscious thought. Sometimes we call this unconscious engagement "being on autopilot."

Being on autopilot does create some efficiencies. When we do the dishes on autopilot, we are less apt to notice or fuss about the fact

---

**Thoughts about Self-Care**

For two to three minutes at a time, practice taking slow, even, deep, relaxed breaths. Some people like to count slowly as they inhale (1 . . . 2 . . . 3 . . .) and then do the same as they exhale (1 . . . 2 . . . 3 . . .). Others prefer to focus simply on slowly inhaling until the inhale feels complete, then slowly exhaling until the exhale feels complete. Another suggestion is to imagine breathing as you would when you are lying down and ready to go to sleep at bedtime. However we do it, this kind of breathing helps our body to unhook from its hardwired stress response with its urgent call to action. It releases us from the hypervigilance and reactivity of stress and frees us to be relaxed and thoughtful as we consider how to respond to the world around us.

A method to counter the physiological and reactive features of stress is called Mindfulness Based Stress Reduction (MBSR). It includes practices such as relaxed breathing and meditation. To learn more about MBSR, visit the Center for Mindfulness in Medicine, Health Care, and Society at the University of Massachusetts Medical School (https://www.umassmed.edu/cfm/mindfulness-based-programs). Classes, groups, books and courses about MBSR are widely available.

that the refrigerator also needs cleaning and the kitchen sink drain is running slow. But sometimes, being on autopilot keeps us from noticing when our habits are not serving us so well. Activities that were once enjoyable, meaningful, and important may have lost those qualities. On autopilot, we might not notice this.

Especially in the midst of grief, your old routine may not be serving you well. Your old routine may not include the rest, nurture, reassurance, and support you *now* need. You may find it impossible to derive the same enjoyment, meaning, and importance from activities that once populated your old routine.

An antidote to living on autopilot is to *consciously* choose what activities will fill your day. Your old routine can still serve as a menu of options, but you can be intentional about choosing from among these options. For example, your old habit may have been to spend time with friends or family nearly every day. If you now find yourself craving more alone time, then make that choice. The opposite might be true for those whose habits tended toward being alone most of the time, but who are now craving the support of others. If this is the case for you, then seek out friends and family more often.

Start your day consciously. When you get up in the morning, notice whether you are looking forward to the day before you. If you are, be curious about the activities or people that seem to lend the day some interest. If not, reflect on what your day is lacking, and add that in. This act of noticing and reflecting is a tool to help you consciously create a routine that provides the nurture and interest you need. When you are not enthused about your day, that day is likely missing something important that you need.

However, if you find yourself feeling *regularly* ambivalent about the day ahead of you, and if (over the course of many days) you have a hard time imagining anything that seems interesting, nurturing or enjoyable, you might be experiencing a form of depression. This is worth your attention.

Many children and adults experience depression during their lifetime, and depression is especially prevalent when major stressors (such as grief) are present. Depression is not a sign that one is failing at self-care, or has less faith than one "should," or just isn't trying hard enough. These myths or stigmas are unhelpful and untrue. There is no shame in being depressed.

If you think you may be depressed, practice all the self-care and stress management habits available to you. In addition, seek medical care—including the use of appropriate medications when advised.

When you are not enthused about your day, that day is likely missing something important that you need.

Symptoms of persistent depressive disorder can cause significant impairment and may include[4]:

- Loss of interest in daily activities
- Sadness, emptiness, or feeling down
- Hopelessness
- Tiredness and lack of energy
- Low self-esteem, self-criticism, or feeling incapable
- Trouble concentrating and trouble making decisions
- Irritability or excessive anger
- Decreased activity, effectiveness, and productivity
- Avoidance of social activities
- Feelings of guilt and worries over the past
- Poor appetite or overeating
- Sleep problems

https://www.mayoclinic.org/diseases-conditions/persistent-depressive-disorder/symptoms-causes/syc-20350929

The chemistry of the human brain is complicated, and sometimes chemical imbalances are at work with depression. So when symptoms of depression appear, take them seriously and get all the help (and all the forms of help) you need.

## Faith

Faith can be a great source of strength and hope in times of sorrow. We propose that faith is grown over a lifetime. We define it as what we've been taught about God and God's relationship with us, combined with what we have come to believe based on our own experiences and thoughtful discernment. As we make our way through life, we will integrate the legacy of faith we've received in a way that makes sense to us.

People of faith have long struggled with the question of suffering. Even those of us who were regular attenders in Sunday school and confirmation class did not spend much time considering the nature of human suffering. We don't spend much time talking about suffering in the larger culture either, so we are understandably ill equipped to see God at work in suffering, especially if we haven't experienced much loss in our lives. If you have not come up with an explanation for suffering that satisfies you, your faith may not be able to offer the kind of support you need when you are facing the loss of a child. There are two common hurdles that can keep faith from being the source of strength and hope you need it to be.

### *Faith as Formula*

The first hurdle is imagining that we need to be perfectly trusting, committed, and confident in our relationship with God at all times. If this is what we expect of ourselves, we may say things like "I *shouldn't* be so impatient," "I *should* have more faith," and "I *shouldn't* be so discouraged."

We have accepted the message that the stories of the Bible show us the mistakes of others to help us avoid making them ourselves. That way, we assume, our practice of faith will be more perfect and less

There is no shame in being depressed.

When symptoms of depression appear, take them seriously and get all the help (and all the forms of help) you need.

flawed than theirs. For this reason, you may think you need to do better than the disciples in the boat who were worried and anxious when the storm came up while Jesus remained asleep. After all, didn't Jesus say to these disciples: "Why are you afraid, you of little faith?" (Matthew 8:26). This sounds like a judgment from Jesus, so why wouldn't we want to do better? Why wouldn't we want to be perfectly calm and trusting in the "storms" we face in life? But what do we do with ourselves when we fail to sail confidently and calmly though this grief?

In Genesis 3:8, we read about Adam and Eve's response to God after they had eaten the fruit that God told them not to eat. When they heard God's voice, they hid themselves. And when they finally did speak to God, they didn't want to report what they had done. Their fear got in the way of a felt sense of closeness with God. So, too, you might hide yourself from God if and when you think a person of faith should not feel as abandoned and despairing as you do. Whether you feel afraid of God because of something you've done wrong or because of how you feel, the practice of hiding from or not wanting to tell God how you feel keeps you from experiencing God's forgiveness, grace, and love.

It's in this honest desire to be good at faith that we run into the hurdle. We too quickly forget that the Bible is primarily a book about God's faithfulness to us, not the other way around. God was faithful to those biblical characters when all was said and done.

When we can turn our attention back to God's love, we can see the gift of faith. God loves us are we are—as impatient, wary, angry, and full of doubt as we might be while struggling to make sense of our loss. In the light of God's love, we can begin to trust that our feelings are normal and that God welcomes them, too.

Telling God exactly what we feel and think takes courage. Yet each time we offer up our whole selves in prayer, we learn to trust that God loves us just the way we are. We learn that God doesn't expect us to feel other than we do. And we learn that if there's any other

> If there's any other way to think or feel about our situation, it has to begin with where we actually are right now.

way to think or feel about our situation, it has to begin with where we actually are right now.

Similarly, the spiritual director William A. Barry speaks of the essence of prayer as standing before God just as we are. He calls this being "transparent" before God.[5] Barry encourages us to present ourselves to God without pretense, hiding nothing. When and as we do this, we come to trust that God loves and is committed to us with the full knowledge of who we really are.

### Faith as Transaction

Though the idea is heartbreaking, many mothers wonder if their baby died because of something they did or didn't do. And this can lead to the second hurdle: wondering if our children died as some form of punishment. After all, the Bible says that God punished King David, who had committed adultery and murder, by causing one of his sons to become ill and die (see 2 Samuel 12:14-19).

People of faith have often thought of God as one who rewards good behavior and punishes wrongdoing. This point of view casts our relationship with God as transactional: if we are good, we are rewarded, and if we are bad, we are punished. In the Gospel of John (9:1-41), we read about a blind man Jesus healed. The story begins with the disciples asking Jesus about the man's condition: "Who sinned, this man or his parents that he was born blind?" Along with our New Testament forebears, we worry at some level that the things we've done wrong may bring God's judgment.

However, Jesus responds, "Neither this man nor his parents sinned; he was born blind so that God's works might be revealed in him." Jesus's words surprised the disciples, who were culturally

William Barry is a Jesuit and has held leadership roles in his denomination in addition to teaching. He has written fifteen books and supported the spiritual formation of many religious leaders in his care. You can learn more about him in the material about "twenty-first-century voices" on the Ignatian Spirituality website (https://tinyurl.com/y9dmcmzj).

conditioned to think illness was always a sign of God's punishment for sin. His words in John 9 served then and now serve as a timeless declaration: Your child did not die because of anyone's sin—not yours or your baby's!

However, while Jesus's words are powerfully reassuring, they still leave an important question outstanding: Then why *did* my child die? And what a question it is. The Old Testament book of Job wrestles with the why of suffering and death. There seems to be no simple or singular answer to this question. Theologians continue to ask it.

We have come to this understanding about the loss of our Erin: We trust Jesus's words that Erin did not die as punishment for her sin or ours. And we now think the reason Erin died is that she was mortal. We don't understand why God chose to create us (in this lifetime) as mortal beings. But we know that as mortal beings, composed of flesh and blood, we are always vulnerable to that which can injure, cripple, or kill us. Therefore, infection and disease can as easily visit babies as they can older adults. Accidents can occur at any age. In faith, we now believe that even in the world that God made and loves, all life is precarious, precious, and finite.

As maturing adults, we will seek to understand why suffering and death are part of life. This would happen even if our children had not died, but we whose children have died are forced to face this question early and often. We urge you to be transparent with God in your seeking. Let God see you wrestle with these questions; invite God into the midst of your struggle. Consider, too, that it may be the wrestling itself that proves the most helpful. That is, when you

Christianity isn't the only spiritual tradition that reminds us that we are mortal. Beginning in prehistory, the Celtic pagan tradition celebrated Beltane (which has evolved into our cultural celebration of May Day). Beltane rituals recognized not just the fertile potential of the coming summer but also the heightened vulnerability of tender young plants and animals to spring's unpredictable weather. Rituals and stories were meant to keep people alert to the fact that life is always precarious.

When you talk with God about all your whys and hows and what-ifs and why-nots, you will experience God's gracious encouragement and love in this process. In so doing, you may find the blessing and the closeness you were really seeking all along.

Those who are marginalized in our society often eloquently capture the pathos of grief because of their own experiences of rejection or oppression.

talk with God about all your whys and hows and what-ifs and why-nots, you will experience God's gracious encouragement and love in this process. In so doing, you may find the blessing and the closeness you were really seeking all along.

## For Caregivers

Early sections of this chapter talk about finding hope in rituals and artistic (written, visual, or musical) expressions. Rituals are designed to help us create structure around transitions that are emotionally powerful. Artists' vocations are all about giving expression to deeply felt emotion. If a piece of music, poetry, or visual art feels as if it was created as a response to suffering or grief, it likely was. If you know authors, songwriters, artists, or poets who have their own story of depression, grief, violence, hardship, or trauma, expect that their work will more likely resonate with people who are grieving. Notice when you are moved, and share the work with grieving friends if they seem open to it. You might even offer a word about how it touched you.

Those who are marginalized in our society often eloquently capture the pathos of grief because of their own experiences of rejection or oppression. Remember to also look at the edges of society for voices that are authentic, powerful, and deeply honest about life's harshness.

This chapter has been about coping skills, and we suggest you reflect on it based on your own purposes. As a caregiver, you have your own grief about this death even as you try to support someone you care about in their grief. You will be doing your own coping.

Becoming familiar with coping skills also allows you to affirm your friends for any advances they make in growing their own coping skills. Remember that people develop coping skills in response to the challenges they have faced. Your grieving friends' coping skills, however well formed they are, may be lacking in ways that are uniquely important for coping with grief. So even if you've seen these friends get through other tough times, don't assume they are prepared for this time of grief.

Expect your grieving friends will need to supplement their coping with new skills and new perspectives. Affirm and encourage their efforts. When they have found a new skill or perspective they want to practice, help them do it. Hold them accountable, if you can do this gently. You could say to them, for example, "You mentioned that practicing yoga a few times a week might be helpful. Have you tried? Is it making a difference for you?"

You could try to notice when they are simply trying to power through life. In this case, you could choose to say, "You seem to be so busy. How is your energy holding up?"

Keep your eyes open for signs of depression. If you notice such signs, you could choose to mirror back to your friend, "This seems to be an especially rough time for you. Is this something that it would be helpful to talk about?"

Whatever question you ask or observation you make, retain a posture of curiosity, not judgment (see chapter 2). See your role as supporting their growing awareness of what they need and their development of the coping skills to meet those needs.

Finally, try to view grief as a catalyst for life-changing and life-enhancing growth. Notice that grief's gifts can include increased compassion and empathy for those who are hurting and the invitation to live life with more intention.

## For Reflection and Discussion

### *For Bereaved Parents*

Talk with someone about these questions.

1  When have you needed to find hope in the past? What offered you the hope that you would get through those rough times?

> Expect your grieving friends will need to supplement their coping with new skills and new perspectives.

> Whatever question you ask or observation you make, retain a posture of curiosity, not judgment.

Try to view grief as a catalyst for life-changing and life-enhancing growth.

2 What has given you hope in this current time of grief? If you need more hope, where might you look for it?

3 Think of someone you know who has experienced great suffering. What do you admire about them? What beliefs and habits of theirs might you want to develop for yourself?

4 Do you like yourself when you feel weak, tired, confused, or ambivalent? If not, what might help you to like yourself even then?

5 How is your faith changing during this time of grief? What questions are you wrestling with right now?

## For Caregivers

This time, your questions are virtually the same as for the bereaved parents.

1 When have you needed to find hope in the past? What offered you the hope then that you would get through those rough times?

2 What gives you hope to face the challenges in your current life? And if you need more hope, where might you look for it?

3 Think of someone you know who has experienced great suffering. What do you admire about them? What beliefs and habits of theirs might you want to develop for yourself?

4 Do you like yourself when you feel weak, tired, confused, or ambivalent? If not, what might help you to like yourself even then?

5 How is your faith changing during this time of grief? What questions are you wrestling with right now?

# Resources

## *Articles*

American Psychological Association. *Is Willpower a Limited Resource?* APA Psychology Help Center, https://tinyurl.com/ycgo4nx4.

> This article about the limits of willpower includes other resources for reference.

Better Health Channel. "Death of a Baby." Department of Health & Human Services, State Government of Victoria, Australia, updated August 2014, https://tinyurl.com/yaytr8rd.

> This post addresses many of the ways babies die and common parental responses.

Goldberg, Joseph. "Dysthymia (Mild, Chronic Depression)." WebMD, February 2017, https://tinyurl.com/y9te7klf.

> A summary of facts about mild, chronic depression.

Mojab, Cynthia Good. "Pregnancy Loss and Infant Death: Understanding Grief and Trauma." Revised. Lynnwood, WA: LifeCircle Counseling and Consulting, 2014, available at https://tinyurl.com/yaxg63uz.

> This brief article is especially useful in making the distinction between grief and depression.

## *Books*

Barry, William A. *God and You: Prayer as a Personal Relationship.* Mahway, NJ: Paulist, 1987.

> Barry presents God as lovingly approachable and suggests ways to pray that are simple, clear, and powerful.

Frankl, Viktor. *Man's Search for Meaning.* Boston: Beacon, 2006.

> Writing in 1946 after his imprisonment in a concentration camp (Auschwitz), Frankl explores how the meaning we assign to our experiences shapes the way we live out our lives.

Hahn, Thich Nhat. *The Miracle of Mindfulness.* Boston: Beacon, 1987.
———. *Peace Is Every Step: The Path of Mindfulness in Everyday Living.* New York: Bantam, 1991.

> Hahn is a Vietnamese Buddhist monk who teaches about mindfulness by telling stories about what we can learn through the ordinary experiences of life.

Kabat-Zinn, Jon. *Wherever You Go, There You Are: Mindfulness Meditation in Everyday Life.* New York: Hachette, 2005.

> Kabat-Zinn introduces the concept of mindfulness and then teaches the reader effective ways to practice it.

Mitchell, Stephen, ed. *The Selected Poetry of Rainer Maria Rilke.* New York: Vintage International, 1989.

> Mitchell translates from German into English selected poems of Rilke. Mitchell includes Rilke's poem "The Tenth Elegy," which invites the reader to meet grief as one would meet a wise elder.

# 4

# What Do I Make of Life after This?

IN THE first months after your child died, grief likely felt like something that was happening *to* you. Grief took over. Whatever plans you had made about life and family were devastated. This experience can cause you to wonder if you should ever make plans, since nothing is guaranteed and all can be undone in a sudden instant.

Some would say that bad things happen in threes. Is that true? No, but it does capture the "waiting for the next shoe to fall" feeling we have when grief is acute. As you and your grief spend more time together, however, you will slowly realize that not everything you hope for falls apart. You will begin to recover your confidence that devastating misfortune and tragedy are not likely to keep striking you down. And you may find yourself inclined to make plans and dream again about your future.

## Making Decisions Again (Big and Small)

Once you are past the first acute stage of grief, you may notice that you are slowly recovering a sense of personal agency—a sense that you are the author of your life. You begin to regain (just enough) energy and hope to make choices about your life. You may start small, planning a little trip or making small changes to your home. In time, you will again ponder life-changing choices. For many, the biggest choice is whether to try to have another child (which we'll talk about later).

Common wisdom about grief says to refrain from making any major decisions about your life for one year. It's as though too much is going on during that first year. Your capacity for careful, strategic, long-range deliberation is overwhelmed by the immediacy of grief. This is likely good advice. However, because your grief is so big, you may feel you need to do something big to respond to it.

David decided to buy a large upright piano shortly after our daughter's death. He was determined to learn to play piano as a therapeutic practice to help with his grief. He spent $300 on this purchase, but the piano turned out to be mostly a piece of furniture (which we paid to have hauled away before our next move). David would call this purchase well intended but not well thought out. Such are the fits and starts of decision-making in the first year after the death of your child.

There's no way to create a road map for year one of grief, because we are making it up as we go. After the first year, there are some quandaries most grieving parents will face. As we get out the house more and more, we'll surely run into situations that reveal just how much life has changed.

## Responding to Strangers

For example, imagine that you are checking out at a grocery or department store and the cashier launches into small talk by asking, "Do you have any children?" How do you answer? This question is often posed with the same intention as "How are you?" Depending on the person asking, it can almost be meant as a rhetorical question. But what should your small-talk response be when your story is anything but small talk?

In a public setting with people you don't know, it can feel awkward and too intimate to say, "I just gave birth to a child who died," or, "I just miscarried." Yet it can feel just as awkward to make a reply that does not acknowledge this child you are missing so much. If this kind of question were rare, maybe you could let it go, but it actually happens fairly often. So what kind of response will honor the truth about your situation while not leaving you feeling too vulnerable or creating too much awkwardness for those around you? Whatever response you choose is important, because it honors not only the life of your child who died but also the way you want to carry their life with you.

This question was especially challenging for us because we were not just grieving our daughter's death, but also the death of raising twins. When we were in public with our surviving twin, we would sometimes be asked, "Do you have any other children?" Early on, especially before our third daughter was born, we would say something like this: "It's our privilege to be Cara's parents."

Now, decades later, we are still often asked how many children we have, and we have settled on saying, "We have had the privilege of raising two daughters." This is true, and we think it's an appropriate response in a passing exchange. If the situation is not simply small talk, or the questioner senses our careful framing and inquires further, we share more. It remains important to us to acknowledge our firstborn daughter's life, as short as it was. She is our daughter, and we are her parents. That's not past tense. We continue to be grateful to have opportunities to say we are the parents of three daughters.

### The Baby's Things

Though you might not think of it as particularly public, you will face another decision about what to do with the baby's room and any baby things you acquired during the pregnancy. Do you leave things as they are, or do you take them down and put them away? Some parents take things down because it feels too painful to leave them as they are. Other parents leave things up and visit that room

> She is our daughter, and we are her parents. That's not past tense.

---

**Thoughts about Self-Care**

Spend some time thinking about how to answer the how-many-children question. If you have no other children, what will you say? Perhaps, "We aren't raising children." If you do, how might you frame it? Honor your own need to acknowledge your child in some way. Perhaps you will just go ahead and say, "We had one child, and we continue to grieve his/her death."

whenever they want a good cry; their grief feels safe and welcome there.

Especially if you aren't juggling the demands of parenting other children, this decision may seem more than you want to take on, especially early on. Or if you had not gotten far in your preparations, it may be one you wish you could struggle with. If you hope to bring a subsequent child into the family soon, perhaps part of your task is to discern how to preserve the memory of your child who died, while changing up the nursery for the sake of a new and different baby. Hopes and dreams are tied up in these preparations!

Eventually, you will likely start making decisions about what artifacts you will reserve for the sake of revisiting your loss and reminding you of your child. In some cultures, families create household shrines to elders who have gone before. Why couldn't you create a small box of things that help you remember your child? You might tuck away a piece of clothing, a picture, the page of that month's calendar, a baptismal certificate, a list of memories, and so forth.

## How You Present Yourself

The next decision may strike you as odd or antiquated—namely, how you choose to dress or look in your grief. King David and the elders put on "sackcloth and ashes" in response to Absalom's death (2 Chronicles 21:16). Sackcloth was worn as an indicator of grief in both the Old and New Testaments. Wearing sackcloth was a sign to all that the wearer was in grief. In many contemporary cultures, grieving persons dress in a particular way for a set period of time. A remnant of this practice is seen today in those who dress in black (or sometimes just wear a black armband) while in grief.

Though you may not be conscious of it, the way you present yourself in public may have changed following the death of your child. You may skip the trouble of applying makeup some days. You may choose more often to dress down or to wear plain, somber-colored clothing. Maybe you go days without shaving or styling your hair.

You could point to these personal-appearance changes and say you just don't have the energy to do anything different. Yet your clothing or makeup choices may also derive from an instinct to wear your grief in such a manner that it reminds others that you had a child who died. *You* are visible to everyone around you. Your child is not. People are not likely to forget that you exist. They are very likely to forget that your child existed. So your choice of clothing and appearance, for a time, will be intertwined with the child you want to remember and want others to remember. Dress accordingly, and trust that however you choose to look is right for you.

### Filling Your Time

What activities you choose to reengage is another personal decision that may also feel like a public statement about your grief. Attending a grief support group, walking alone in the park, going to church, reading a book at home—these kinds of activity probably feel congruent with your grief. Behaviorally, they may feel a bit like wearing a black armband.

But, what if you choose to go dancing or golfing, or to attend a movie or a concert? How might that look to others? How might that feel to you?

While there's no harm in doing any of these things, you are likely to experience them, at least at first, as a bit jarring. You may notice that you don't find the usual pleasure or meaning in these activities. For example, you might once have spent all week eagerly looking forward to dancing on Friday night, and now it might feel like a chore. You may even feel a sense of anticipatory dread or apprehension at the thought of going out dancing again.

Some of this apprehension can arise from anticipating what others might expect of you. You might guess that companions could exert some pressure on you (intended or not) to act just as you used to do. For example, if you were the life of the party or the wild one or the playful one, you might feel an expectation to be like that again. You might even get the impression that they think this is good for you—as if it might help you shake off your grief.

Furthermore, in these social situations, you might feel pressure to not spoil the gathering with your grief and instead to join wholeheartedly in the fun. In addition, you may worry that when you do reengage these former favorite activities, it could imply to your friends that you're done grieving and are back to being your good old self. So many nuances! Why is this so hard?

Know and accept that sometimes you *do* need a distraction or a break from the intensity of your grief. Going bowling or dancing or seeing a movie may be the perfect thing to do once in a while. But also notice when an activity feels too emotionally complicated or when you feel as if you have to leave your grief behind in order to engage in it.

Grief has a habit of showing up unannounced. It goes everywhere you do. So it will as easily visit you at the bowling alley as in your baby's room. The fact that you feel moments of sadness when bowling is not a bad thing. The problem arises when you weren't expecting it and were hoping it would stay away. Trust that your grief isn't trying to spoil your fun. It's just reminding you that the person bowling (you) is also a person whose child died. Sometimes the juxtaposition of those two realities (like hot and cold air masses colliding) produces a bit of an emotional storm.

> Apprehension can arise from anticipating what others might expect of you.

> Sometimes you *do* need a distraction or a break from the intensity of your grief.

## Thoughts about Self-Care

Look at your activity decisions as an experiment. Try one out, and then reflect on how it went. For example, go bowling. If it was fun, try it again. If this time you come home in tears, reflect on what was different. The expectations of others can make a difference, but so can the expectations you place on yourself. It might be that you really wanted this activity to be fun again (you really needed a break from your grief), but seeing a pregnant woman bowling two lanes over kept reminding you of your grief.

Grief has a habit
of showing up
unannounced.

You will get more
and more used to the
coexistence of play and
grief, of work and grief,
of holidays and grief, of
activities and grief.

The activities you
choose to reengage
will often reflect a
greater intention and
urgency to do what
feels important, and
an awareness of the
preciousness and
finiteness of life.

You will get more and more used to the coexistence of play and grief, of work and grief, of holidays and grief, of activities and grief. You will learn how to carry both at once, though that will take time. And it is very likely you will reprioritize your activities to best align with your new reality, your needs, and your values.

David recalls his prior habit of playing golf at least once a week and spending Sunday afternoons watching football. After our daughter's death, these activities felt less important, especially because they took him away from family. Reserving Sunday afternoons for family time quickly became a new habit that provided an abundance of nurture and delight.

Remember that life looks different when you see it through the lens of grief. You no longer assume you have all the time in the world. Activities that are fun but unimportant may lose some or all of their appeal. The activities you choose to reengage will often reflect a greater intention and urgency to do what feels important, and an awareness of the preciousness and finiteness of life. Over time, this will reshape your life. (We'll look at this in more detail in chapter 5.) This new decision-making represents your increasing sense of agency. You are beginning to feel again that you are the author of your life.

### Friends Change as You Change

One consequence of being proactive about these important decisions is that you may find yourself spending more time with one set of friends than with another. If you haven't already, you will notice that some friends or family members are easier to be around than others. You will be inclined to limit time spent with those who don't seem to know how to make room for your grief. You will gravitate toward those who are able to fully welcome you *and* your grief.

This reprioritizing of friendships happens unintentionally at first. Early in your grief, you are simply trying to keep your head above water and will naturally reach out to those who feel like life preservers. But as you gain greater perspective and agency, you will begin to make more conscious choices about who you want to join you for conversation, meals, or activities.

This conscious choosing about who to spend your time with is awkward. Why? Early in your grief, you weren't thinking about whether, say, your bowling buddies would be hurt if you stayed home. But now this might be a concern. Now friends and family might notice if you don't have much contact with them and wonder if something is wrong. That creates awkwardness. Do you tell them that their support isn't very effective?

Your friends and family are unlikely to ask you directly, "Why don't we see you much anymore?" But this question will likely feel present in an unspoken form. Some grieving parents choose to let the question and their "answer" remain unspoken. It doesn't avoid the awkwardness, but it avoids the risk of the difficult conversation you would face if you were to bring it up. Parents often choose this approach if the friends or family members involved were not people they felt especially close to or spent much time with anyway.

What about the relationships that do feel important yet don't feel nurturing in the way you need? If you see some potential for these relationships to be supportive, investing time and energy in them is a good choice. You may be the first in your circle of friends to have faced a traumatic loss, but given the nature of life and aging, you won't be the last. Try welcoming these friends into your experience of grief. Teach them how they might support you. Your welcome and teaching will grow their capacity to support others in grief, including you. Share this book with them, and point out the sections for caregivers. Of course, add any suggestions of your own. The potential gain is a friendship that is deeper, stronger, and more transparent.

You will gravitate toward those who are able to fully welcome you *and* your grief.

## When You Are Both Grieving

Grieving the loss of a child as a couple is even more complicated than navigating grief with family and friends. For some, the gulf that opens up between partners who are grieving differently may lead to separation or even divorce. However, though a higher divorce rate is still presented as a common outcome of the loss of a child, recent studies have indicated that the end of the marriage or partnership is not a given.[1]

Three decades ago, we heard in our support group that 70 percent of couples divorce in the first year after a child dies. Though we have since learned that this statistic was not accurate, it was sobering at the time. Our major decision for that first year was to commit to doing everything we could to avoid that outcome. For us, this included attending a grief support group, getting support from a grief counselor, and eventually, also seeing a marriage counselor. We were especially blessed that the marriage counselor we saw had also lost a twin. Because we shared this common experience, his work with us was even more helpful.

Learn more about what makes relationships strong and enduring. That will serve you well in the years after a child dies. For many young couples, good relationships seem to just happen with little or no effort on their part. The powerful and giddy love that drew them together feels as if it will always be enough to keep them together.

Falling in love, as transporting as it is, is a stage of love, and this stage doesn't usually have the strength you need to support you following the death of your child. The first blushes of love bring us together with our partners. From there, we work bit by bit to build a relationship that nurtures, sustains, inspires, consoles, and even challenges us, so we might become our best selves. Ideally, we would be able to do this work without having to face any devastating stressors too early in our relationships. We need time to be able to slowly build up the strength and vitality of a relationship so that one day it might be able to withstand hardship and tragedy with grace and hope.

Unfortunately, you have experienced the death of a child, likely in the early years of your relationship. Your relationship may lack some of the strengths and trust that can come with more years together. So it's common to worry or at least wonder whether your relationship will survive the death of a child. This is a scary feeling—far removed from the giddiness you felt when falling in love.

You read earlier that participating in a support group or seeing a grief or marriage counselor can help you work through the challenges you face. Depending on the availability or cost of these resources, you can also read (in print or online) anything you find helpful regarding how to build and maintain healthy relationships. The strongest suggestion we have for you is that you talk with one another—about what you are thinking and what you are feeling—and reserve judgment if you can. Stay curious. If you find these conversations don't always go the way you'd like, look for books or articles that help you develop good communication skills.

### Good Communication

The most important thing you can do to support your relationship is to give each other space and time—extra grace. Grief is a powerful stressor. As we noted in chapter 3, stress prompts us to replace thoughtful consideration with instinctive protective responses. Thus, even *thinking* about communicating well can be a struggle.

Good communication assumes that you cannot know what someone is saying until you hear it from *their* perspective. Furthermore, it assumes that the things people say can be like icebergs—that is, their real substance lies hidden under the surface. Your attention to good communication, especially when you have crossed wires together, is an important investment in the long-term health of your relationship.

Consider this example. You come home after work, and your partner assails you with these words: "You did it again. You forgot to take my shirts out of the dryer, so they've been bunched up all day, getting wrinkled. I can't wear them like this! It's so frustrating. I'm getting really tired of your carelessness."

Your first instinct, a natural one, is to get defensive. An inner monologue may start up in your head: "Really!? You're all bent out of shape about a wrinkled shirt? So you can't iron or rewash it? And this is how you want to welcome me home after I've been working hard for us all day?"

From this mind-set, you might respond by telling your partner about something *they've* overlooked that inconvenienced *you*. You might sarcastically explain why you couldn't take the shirts out of dryer before you went to work. Or you might say, "In the grand scheme of life, your wrinkled shirt is so trivial it's not even worth talking about."

We've all been part of conversations like this. They get started on the wrong foot and often continue to devolve until you both feel terrible—mad, confused, depressed, and spent. Apologies may be hard to offer. Hurt feelings may smolder for a while.

While seemingly unavoidable, these conversations leave us thinking that there must be a better way. One example of a "better way" comes from psychologist Daniel Wile, author of *After the Honeymoon: How Conflict Can Improve Your Relationship*.[2] When conversations get all tangled up, Wile proposes that you "do them over." The specifics of his approach go something like this:

- Notice when a conversation is producing hurt feelings, anger, or defensiveness.
- Recall what you said (or heard) that started this chain reaction of feelings.
- Take responsibility for your words and/or reactions.
- Offer a different way of saying what you meant and/or responding to what you heard.

Daniel Wile, PhD, is a Diplomate in Clinical Psychology of the American Board of Professional Psychology. One early review said of his work in *After the Honeymoon*, "What most invigorates this book . . . is Wile's firm grasp and display of sensitive psychological points between partners: the fear of abandonment and of being taken for granted, the resentment of domination, dependency, and boredom that, in fact, are the roots of many conflicts" (*Publishers Weekly*, 1988, https://tinyurl.com/y9gympjn).

While both partners need to understand how this approach works, only one of you needs to initiate it.

Here's how that *might* change the example. The partner coming home from work might say, "Can we start this conversation over? I sure want to. I'm realizing that your words about the wrinkled shirts really set me off *(notice your hurt)*. I had a rough day at work and was looking forward to coming home and getting some sympathy. So when you greeted me with blame, I kind of lost it *(recall what you said or heard)*. I'm sorry *(take responsibility)*. Instead of saying what I did, I wish I would have said, 'I can hear how frustrated you are.' Is there more you want to say about this?" *(offer an alternative approach)*

Hearing this, the partner frustrated by the wrinkled shirts will feel that their concern was heard and may respond, "You know, the wrinkled shirts were frustrating, but what I think I'm most frustrated about is our lack of time together recently. You've been so focused on work that it doesn't feel like I'm important to you right now."

The aim of Wile's approach is to help couples recover from conversational disasters and reclaim their ability to talk meaningfully about what is truly important, such as their shared love for and support of one another.

It should be noted that our example assumes two partners whose shared intention is to build a healthy relationship and who are mutually committed to developing good communication skills. It could also be true that the critical comment about the wrinkled shirts is part of a fault-finding *habit* of a person who has given up on the relationship and wants out. Good communication skills may—in a best-case scenario—help you discover this, but resolving it will take more than good communication. Counseling then is a best next step and may help you discover each partner's willingness to recommit to the relationship.

Good (productive) communication includes validating the feelings that are shared and then being curious about where they came from. If their named source sounds trivial, wonder if something else is at work and not being named. When you respond with curiosity, you presume that there *is* more going on under the surface. Curiosity seeks to engage conversation in a manner that helps it go deeper, not simply flame up at the surface.

Be aware that underneath many critical comments are often unmet and unspoken needs. The needs could be for affection, consolation, reassurance, kindness, closeness, affirmation, or thanks, to name just a few. The need could be for an apology or for forgiveness. It could be the need to know whether your partner is still committed to this relationship and to facing this grief together.

Therefore, be graceful with one another. Grace is a quality often attributed to God, but it is a really important quality in every relationship. Being graceful means realizing that none of us can get it right or behave admirably every time. We are not always at our best. Things *will* come out of our mouth or our partner's mouth that should not have been said or should not have been said that way. Grace is the quality that allows us to love ourselves and our partner even when this happens. And then it will motivate us to find and practice a better way.

As part of our grief work, we adopted the habit of saying, "This is a feeling statement" when we wanted to share something charged with emotion. This tipped off the one listening to expect that what they were about to hear was going to be uncensored. It's odd that this could be helpful, for all it really means is that the one speaking is not going to be careful about choice of words or tone of voice. But this warning somehow seems to give permission to the listener to take the communication with a grain of salt. It helped us listen to the content and not get hooked by the innuendo of the words being spoken. It is a habit we have retained.

Good communication skills are really important and also deceptively difficult to develop and practice. Therefore, give each other permission and encouragement to be slow learners. Agree to fail often at this task until you finally get better at it. Good communication is a foundational skill that will serve again and again to keep your relationship vital and healthy.

Finally, choose to share and discuss concerns when they arise, rather than letting them fester. At first, this could make it seem as if there are more problems in your relationship than there used to be. In time, however, you will come to trust that you are simply being more proactive in addressing the many concerns and hurt feelings that are part and parcel of all relationships.

## Subsequent Children

Even now, you can surely list good reasons for trying to get pregnant (or adopt) again right away, and also for waiting to get pregnant again. Some couples choose to wait. Others don't. One choice is not better than the other. Whatever decision you make is the right one for you. But as you are making this decision, it can be helpful to consider the feelings that are likely to accompany it.

Fear tops the list of these feelings. You recently experienced the death of a child. You can't help but think, "Why wouldn't or couldn't it happen again?" If someone were to tell you that there is less than a 2 percent chance that a subsequent child will die, you would not feel reassured. After all, your child who did die might have had those same odds. A 98 percent chance of living also means a 2 percent chance of dying. Ninety-eight percent is reassuring only when your baby lives.

Fear is the emotion that forces you to seriously consider whether you are prepared to face the death of another child. Without fear, you might enter into a subsequent pregnancy armed only with wishful thinking—the innocent assumption that death will never visit you again. But fear won't allow you to be this innocent. It demands that you consider what could happen if yet another of your children should die.

In this regard, fear is your friend. It won't let you (or tries not to let you) pursue a subsequent child until you're sure you have the support you need should the worst happen. Your child's death blindsided you once. Fear asks that you learn from that experience and make preparations for best- *and* worst-case outcomes.

This fear is enough to cause some parents to wait until they've healed more fully and developed support systems that feel more solid. Some parents don't wait. They trust that the way they are dealing with their grief now is good enough for them to assume they'll do no worse if a subsequent child dies. Either way, parents anticipate that any subsequent pregnancy or adoption process will be marked by fear.

In some communities, there are support groups just for mothers who are pregnant (or are trying to get pregnant) after the death of a child. In these groups, mothers talk about both the joyful anticipation of having another child and their worry that something will go wrong with the pregnancy. This new pregnancy is also a reminder of the pregnancy that preceded it. Therefore, mothers can't help but recall the child that died, even as they now carry a child they hope will live.

We were just into our thirties when our daughter died, and we had endured a difficult pregnancy with the twins. Catherine had spent two months on short-term disability early in the pregnancy with persistent vomiting (hyperemesis gravidarum) and was hospitalized at about twelve weeks after worrisome weight loss and dehydration. It was during that hospitalization that the twins were diagnosed. Our original intent was to have two children, and the complications of the pregnancy made the diagnosis of twins, though daunting, welcome news. When one of our twins died, we realized that we had to decide if we would go through another pregnancy. We decided to do so, but part of moving forward was our own clarity that we needed to be prepared to lose this subsequent child as well.

When Abbie was born, we were simultaneously relieved to have survived another unpleasant pregnancy, thrilled to meet this new person, and terrified that she would die, too. We checked her breathing often, and we faced our fear by learning to put her down for a nap without one of us being there all the time. Though we knew we could lose either of our surviving daughters at any time to any number of dangers, we made a decision that David would have a vasectomy. At Catherine's insistence, however, we did not do this until Abbie was two years and eight days old, the age of the oldest baby we'd heard of who had died of SIDS. This was a small way to have some agency, even though we knew full well that we didn't have control over our own mortality or that of our children. The vasectomy was a decision that there would be no more subsequent children.

The excitement of a subsequent pregnancy will feel somewhat muted. You may wait to tell others about it. Your words about this pregnancy will tend to be careful and cautious. Sometimes friends and family will think this means you are "trying not to get too attached," in case this baby dies. They would be completely wrong about that. You are totally and lovingly attached to this budding new life, and you are also terrified, knowing that they are mortal. In any subsequent pregnancy, notice your feelings—often hope and fear, excitement and worry—and share them with those you love and trust.

One of Catherine's colleagues experienced five miscarriages between the birth of her first child and her second, all within two years (they started trying four years after the birth of their daughter). When her seventh pregnancy had gone on long enough for her to begin to trust that it would go to term, she reported her lingering doubts. Even a month before her son was due, she had not yet set up a nursery. She did eventually prepare a room for him, of course, and she could not be happier that he has taken up residence in her life. But she is quite clear that the grief of so many losses over the two years that preceded his birth really dampened her excitement as she anticipated her son's arrival.

## Rituals of Remembrance

Grief and remembrance walk hand in hand. As time passes, we understandably have a strong desire to remember the children we have lost, even when this comes with feelings of sadness. We don't want them to disappear from our lives. They are too precious and important for us to let that happen.

As parents, we commit ourselves to tending to the lives of our children. We commit to providing for their needs, demonstrating our love for them, introducing them to the wider world, teaching them what we deem important and valuable, and helping them discover who they are and what to do with their lives. This commitment isn't for a day or a month or a year. We make this commitment for the lifetime of our children.

What are we supposed to do with this commitment when a child dies? A major task of grieving is to figure out how to direct this parenting energy in a manner that remembers and honors the child who died. Sadly, some of us didn't have much time to build memories. Many parents who have this experience report worrying about whether those few memories will fade completely.

Early in our grief, there wasn't a day that went by without our daughter Erin being foremost in our thoughts. Yet as time when on, we noticed days when she was not top of mind all the time. We worried whether this trend would continue. After more than three decades, we trust now that we will never forget her. Some of our specific memories are still sharp and clear, but most are less so. We can and do remember, but now we have a little more control over when those memories wash over us. We were also taught by some of our parishioners, women in their eighties and nineties who wept with us over children they had lost sixty and seventy years before. We don't forget; we remember.

Some of us didn't have much time to build memories.

We don't forget; we remember.

Creating and practicing rituals of remembrance supports remembering when we aren't able to raise the children we still love. Some rituals are private and informal. Perhaps you have a toy saved in the corner of a drawer, or a blanket that would have sheltered your baby. When you bring out these keepsakes, they trigger memory. Some rituals are relatively public and formal, such as funerals or memorial services in the immediate aftermath or family gatherings on an anniversary date. Others are more personal.

## Personal Rituals

Personal rituals can be very private or include others. Some may be as simple as handling objects that remind you of your baby. Others may necessitate more planning and preparation. Anything you do that allows you to bring words, your senses, or a feeling of holiness or sacredness will honor and support your memories.

We saved a newborn-size burgundy-colored sleeper, because Erin was often wearing it in the pictures we have of her. It was a hand-me-down from her cousin, so it was well used. Its attractiveness is not the point, however. Holding this sleeper still powerfully calls us back to the two-month-old infant who once filled it out.

What kind of keepsakes will do? This is an especially important question if you were never able to hold your child. Almost anything can work, because you are the one who will impart memory to the object, not the other way around. Choose anything that will trigger your senses, especially smell or touch and even sound. Handling these objects will give you time to pull the memory up. Here are some ideas:

- A maternity top
- The stick from your pregnancy test
- The calendar page that includes the day when your pregnancy was confirmed, the day you heard there was a child for you (adoption), or the day you heard your child had died
- A toy you bought anticipating your child's arrival, especially if it makes a noise of some kind

- A sheet from the crib
- A receiving blanket (even if it never held your child, you can claim it as one that would have)
- The birth certificate with foot imprints
- A stuffed animal with your child's name
- A beautiful stone

If you have them, pictures also can serve to carry memory. Periodically take time to review pictures of your child. Each captures a moment in time and can help you both recall and tell the story of your child. Display these pictures in your home and revisit them. Occasionally someone will notice and ask about them—a chance to tell the story (if the situation is right) and to remember once again.

Pictures can also be something drawn by surviving children or by you or other loved ones. This can be done even if you never actually saw your child. You can choose an image that represents this precious one. Again, you are the one who imparts memory to these things.

After our daughter's funeral, we made a scrapbook to help us remember. We included pictures of Erin taken in the weeks she was with us, plus copies of the baby shower invitation, birth announcements from a variety of sources, the wrist bands Catherine and Erin wore in the hospital, the little card with her name and statistics from her hospital bassinet, the tiny hat she wore home from the hospital, her birth certificate, a copy of her obituary, the funeral service bulletin and sermon, sympathy cards that were especially meaningful, and poems written by Catherine and friends. Our daughters were baptized soon before Erin died, so we also included Erin's baptismal certificate and the towel used to dry her head. We have continued to add things over the years. The scrapbook isn't fancy, and many items are simply tucked in between pages.

We have a habit of revisiting the scrapbook on the anniversary of Erin's death. Sometimes we two parents do this alone together. On the thirtieth anniversary of her death, we invited our surviving daughters and future son-in-law to join us in this review.

In addition to keepsakes you can pull out on occasion, you may want to have a keepsake you carry as a matter of course. Some bereaved parents buy a necklace or bracelet that has a charm for each of their children, including the baby who died. Wearing this jewelry is an act of remembering that invites storytelling when others comment on the number of children represented by the charms. Some parents get a tattoo to remember the baby who died—footprints, a name, or some other image that represents the baby.

Especially for those who experience miscarriage, choosing a name for your baby can be an act of remembering. Some parents name their baby many years after their child's death. Some find that naming a miscarried baby is a way to make the loss more tangible. Name your baby if and when it feels right to you.

## Shared Remembering

Remembering in more public ways can be powerful, because community is so important to helping us grieve. Other people experienced this loss, too, and are with us as we navigate our loss. They remember and become carriers of memory. Creating opportunities to share and tell those stories can be very healing, especially as the years go by.

If you have a yard, you could plant a tree or shrub or flowers in memory of your child. If you don't have a yard, you could purchase a special houseplant for your home or plant a tree or purchase a bench for a public garden, park, or church yard. You can do this quietly and without a formal or public ritual. But you could also gather family and friends to dedicate the planting or bench and continue to meet over the subsequent years.

Our surviving twin experienced a miscarriage between the births of our two grandchildren. She and her husband invited us to be with them in their backyard as they planted a magnolia tree in memory of this baby we would never know. They chose a magnolia because it would bloom every year at about the time of the miscarriage and their loss.

Before the tree was set in the hole, they placed in it the placenta from their son's birth (it had long been sitting in their freezer) and the tissue remains from the miscarriage, which they had requested before her D&C procedure. We offered some words together, remembering our sadness about the child who was lost and gratitude for our grandson, who was thriving. We offered a prayer of thanks for the miracle and privilege of being parents and asked the Spirit to bear us up in our grief about this loss.

Rather than plant a tree, some choose to create a memorial garden. It might be big or small, even in a pot. It could include obvious markers with a name (more like a cemetery) or not. The important thing is setting aside this space as a place to remember. The beauty of these efforts can evoke a celebration of life amidst the grief.

Candles are a simple and more portable symbol of remembrance. Think of lighting a candle when you want to be intentional about remembering your child (in your own home or in the home of family or friends). At a time of your choosing, light the candle in honor of your child, and speak his or her name. If your child was baptized in a congregational ceremony and you were given a baptismal candle to take home, you can remember the fulfillment of the baptismal promises made by God and light the baptismal candle. Even in solo moments of silence with candles that have no particular significance, lighting a candle can center the moment, and the flame can symbolize the presence and memory of your child.

### Marking Anniversaries

You will be the best judge of what anniversaries to commemorate. You may want to remember the day your pregnancy was confirmed or, if adopting, the day you found out there was a child for you. You may want to remember the due date, the birth date, the arrival date of an adopted child, or the death date. Especially early on, many choose to mark all of these in some way. It's likely that eventually you will settle on one or two days in the year to make a habit of remembering.

First anniversaries deserve special mention and care. As a first anniversary approaches, don't be surprised if your grief feels especially intense, raw, and overwhelming. This will be unsettling, given that you may have experienced a bit of energy returning and found some initiative coming back as the months go by. Then, as that first anniversary approaches, many feel like grief is taking over again, much as it did when it was brand new. For this reason, some parents are surprised by the seeming setback of first anniversaries.

Given the intensity of grief that is likely to accompany first anniversaries, it's good to create a plan for how you will take care of yourself. If at all possible, take the day off from work. If you don't want to be alone, think of which family members or friends you want to join you. Then imagine and choose some ritual act of remembering. You could invite your pastor to help you create a brief memorial service, for example.

If your child was buried, a ritual act could be driving to the cemetery and putting flowers on your child's grave. If your child was cremated, this could be a time to distribute ashes in some sacred place, if that has not already been done. One mother created a "tree" in her living room with hundreds of paper cranes she had folded in memory of her child. She then invited family and friends over to remember her child with her. Some wait until a first anniversary to plant a shrub or a tree in their yard—often something evergreen or flowering. It's not the size or scope of the ritual that is most important, but rather the intention to remember.

Know, too, that your feelings may peak in intensity prior to an anniversary or in the days following it. On the day itself, you may feel emotionally flat or numb. This, of course, is normal. We mention it here primarily so that you can know and expect that the days *around* these anniversaries also may be difficult. Therefore,

It's not the size or scope of the ritual that is most important, but rather the intention to remember.

> Make self-care and support a priority during the time of these first anniversaries.

make self-care and support a priority during the time of these first anniversaries.

We were surprised by the intensity of our emotions on the first anniversary of Erin's death. Over the years, we have come to recognize the time between our daughters' birthday in early October and Erin's death date at the end of November as a time when grief comes to visit with more insistence. We are grateful that our bodies and spirits seem to remember even when we are distracted by the business of life.

## Thoughts about the Sacramental Nature of Remembering

In the Christian tradition, a simple meal is transformed into a holy act of remembrance. Holy Communion, the Eucharist, and the Lord's Supper are all names for the meal that recalls Jesus's sharing bread and wine with his disciples during the time of the Passover celebration. Early Christian interpreters of Jesus's story saw this meal as a key event and experience in the life of the disciples. We are the inheritors of this ritual of remembrance, and many congregations celebrate it weekly.

Another ritual for remembering can be making a donation to a favorite charity. Maybe you have already done this in memory of your child. On an anniversary (also a way to mark holidays), you could ask that others contribute in your child's memory. Some grieving parents organize charity events, like a golf tournament or pizza night, where they raise money for a charity that is connected to their child somehow. Some start a scholarship named for the child. This act of remembering not only honors the child who died, but also benefits the cause(s). Some charities annually generate a list of gifts made in memory of a loved one in the past year. Seeing your child's name on such a list feels good and important. It may feel like the start of a legacy.

You can also remember your child in your estate planning. It might be as simple as a memorial bequest to the organization doing research on the cause of your child's death or an addition from your estate to a scholarship you established in your child's name. Some parents include all of their children as they consider the distribution of their estate. They designate the portion that would have gone to their deceased child as charitable distributions to organizations they care about.

Whenever the sacrament of Holy Communion is celebrated, words (officially, the "Words of Institution") are spoken over the bread and wine, recalling what Jesus said at his last supper with his disciples. You may know some of these words by heart: "This is my body, given for you. . . . This is my blood, shed for you." And you may also recall these words: "Do this in remembrance of me."

In the sacrament of Communion, we are reminded that gifts and blessings can arise out of the death of a loved one. Martin Luther wrote that the sacraments are "a pure, wholesome, soothing medicine which aids and quickens us in both soul and body. For where the soul is healed, the body has benefited also."

Apply this sacramental thinking to the rituals you create to remember your child. First, note that this is different from a funeral ritual. At a funeral, the emphasis is on your struggle with the finality of death and the weight of your initial grief. A funeral happens once. In contrast, the sacrament of Communion is celebrated weekly in many churches. And though it recalls this last supper, its focus is on blessings received from God: God's steadfast presence and nourishment, forgiveness, and reconciliation with God and neighbor.

In the rituals you create, trust that blessings will come from God and from those who surround you with support. Though it may

Jesus's "Last Supper" is described in four places in the New Testament:

- Matthew 26:26–29
- Mark 14:22–25
- Luke 22:14–23
- 1 Corinthians 11:23–26

The frequent biblical retelling is a sure sign of the importance of this remembrance to the faith of early Christians. In fact, most Christian traditions call Holy Communion a sacrament. Martin Luther defines sacraments as "rites which have the command of God, and to which the promise of grace has been added."[3] Many Christians experience grace in Holy Communion. Its comfort is often requested in times of illness, vulnerability, or uncertainty.

seem surprising, blessings also come from your child who is no longer present with you. He or she not only blessed your life during the time you had together, but still blesses you now as you heal and grow.

Sometimes the blessing is "simply" feeling close to and grateful for family members and friends who have been accompanying you on this journey of grief and are willing to participate in these rituals with you. Blessing may also come as a realization that your deep, abiding love for your child is a gift from God and also represents God's love for you ("We love because God first loved us"; 1 John 4:19). If the ritual reveals or calls forth some energy or imagination that was lying dormant for the past several months, this can feel like a blessing. Whatever form they take, look for these blessings, and let them reinforce your intention to remember your child.

## Caring for Yourself

As you move through the first year(s) of grief, you become acutely aware of life's breadth and complexity. In this chapter alone, we've looked at rituals, relationships, communication, appearance, and activities. All of these aspects of life were part of your experience prior to your child's death, but you may be seeing them in a new light on this side of your child's death.

Grief tends to open our eyes to many more aspects of life than we may have paid attention to before. Those who grieve now notice others who are in grief. We now notice more feelings, when previously we might have ignored many of them. We notice interpersonal awkwardness with family, friends, and colleagues. We notice how we look, what we eat, what we think, and how much energy we have. Initially, to notice so much feels overwhelming.

So what to do about this? Creating some kind of system to help you pay attention to what's important can be helpful. On the adjoining page is a sample of an inventory that David created for his use during the first year of our grieving and that you may find useful.

> Look for these blessings, and let them reinforce your intention to remember your child.

You may copy this page or freely change and adapt the tool to meet your personality, preferences, and needs.

The point of creating and using a self-assessment tool like this is to help you pay attention to your practice of self-care. It helps you notice what you are doing well and what might be missing. While all of the categories in the sample are potentially meaningful, you will likely assign more importance to some than to others. Choose categories that are meaningful and important to *you*.

If tracking these categories of self-care each week feels like a chore, do it less often or just randomly. For example, if you had an especially good week or an especially hard week, you might use this inventory to look for clues. Learn which forms of self-care seem to be essential for your sense of well-being, and do your best to practice these each week. In time, this monitoring will become ingrained, and your best self-care practices will become a habit. Until then, be mindful and intentional about your self-care, so you are best able to engage all that is important to you.

## For Caregivers

Read this poem by Kathleen Sheeder Bonanno:[5]

**What People Give You**

Long-faced irises. Mums.
Pink roses and white roses
and giant sunflowers,
and hundreds of daisies.

Fruit baskets with muscular pears,
and water crackers and tiny jams
and the steady march of casseroles.
And money,
people give money these days.

Another tool you can use to assess your overall well-being is the Wholeness Wheel, used by the Evangelical Lutheran Church in America to talk about wellness. You can find it on the Portico Benefit Services website at https://tinyurl.com/ybj8vm7h.

## Self-Assessment Inventory

Week of _____

### Well-Being

On a scale of 1–10, where 1 means no agreement with the statement and 10 means full agreement, rate each aspect of your well-being.

_____ Emotional: I seek the inspiration to be hopeful, engaged, and content.

_____ Spiritual: I feel connected to self, world, and God, and I have a clear sense of purpose.

_____ Physical: I make time for aerobic activity and for flexibility and strength training.

_____ Nutritional: My diet is a healthy balance of the major food groups.

_____ Social: I seek out sufficient and quality time with friends and family.

_____ Intellectual: I seek to be informed and to engage in discussion and reflection.

_____ Recreational: I make time for activities that nurture, inspire, delight, and challenge me.

_____ Rest/renewal: I get adequate sleep and find time for self-care.

_____ Charitable: I spend time and/or money to help others in need.

_____ Vocational: I'm proud of the ways I invest myself in school, work, and volunteering.

### Family, Friend, and Peer Relationships

Record the dates and main topics of significant and memorable interactions.

| Date | Topic |
| --- | --- |
| _____ | _____ |
| _____ | _____ |
| _____ | _____ |
| _____ | _____ |
| _____ | _____ |

Cards, of course:
the Madonna, wise
and sad just for you,
Chinese cherry blossoms,
sunsets and moonscapes,
and dragonflies for transcendence.

People stand by your sink
and offer up their pain:
Did you know I lost a baby once,
or My eldest son was killed,
or My mother died two months ago.

People are good.

They file into your cartoon house until it bows at the seams;
they give you every
blessed
thing,
everything,
except your daughter back.

Hopefully you hear in this poem both commendation for the
wonderful, important, and loving things you can do as a caregiver
and also a cautionary word about the one thing your support
cannot do. This both/and is what most caregivers (and partners, too)
find so challenging. You can be at your loving best, and still the grief
stubbornly remains in the one you are trying to care for and love.
No amount of love can change this reality: a child has died. You
cannot lessen the grief that accompanies such a death. When you
offer your expressions of love with this awareness, they will have a

Kathleen Bonnano's daughter was murdered by an ex-boyfriend. This poem is in her book *Slamming Open the Door*, a collection of poetry expressing her responses. For more about the author and book, see Terry Gross, "On the Page, Poet Mourns Daughter's Murder," *Fresh Air*, July 29, 2009, https://tinyurl.com/y9cn4jhv.

No amount of love can change this reality: a child has died.

powerful impact—far more than if you offered them as some kind of cure for grief.

As you read the section on major decisions, you surely noticed the discussion of relationships. We noted there that grieving parents usually spend less and less time with family members and friends who are not able to hold open some space for their grief. The fact that you're reading this book makes it highly likely that you are the kind of family member or friend that grieving parents cherish and value. It's also likely that you feel as if there is still so much you don't yet know or understand about grief.

You can't hurry this learning process, so you often will not be able to engage another's grief with all the understanding that you might wish you had. What you *can* do is choose to be vulnerable and dive in anyway. The courage it takes to do this is not lost on those who are grieving.

You may recall our discussion of empathy versus sympathy in chapter 2. Sympathy tends to be the stance of people who know a lot about grief and want to share that knowledge with those who are grieving. Empathy is the stance taken by people (who may or may not know a lot about grief) who choose simply to be with and listen to the person who is grieving. Sympathy tends to stand above, like a teacher. Empathy stands *with* another and demonstrates love by its willingness to be vulnerable. Empathy is the preferred response.

When your grieving friends slowly regain energy and agency, think carefully about how you might call attention to this. For example, if you said to them, "It's so great to see you acting more like your old self," this could imply that you prefer this person's old self to their grieving self. Instead, try saying, "You seem to have more energy today," and then listen to whatever they have to say about this. Their interpretation, not yours, is what's important here.

In the section on sacramental aspects of remembering, we proposed that grief can beget blessings—not just pain, suffering, sadness, and weariness, but blessing. Grief can be a gift, just as the child who died was and is a gift. A common error that caregivers make is to assume that grief and a happy, productive life are mostly incompatible. Grief is imagined to be like a snowstorm that makes car travel treacherous, so we need to stay home until the snow melts and then celebrate that it's gone. Please, don't think of grief like that. And don't make responses that celebrate grief's seeming absence.

Grief is at heart about the enduring presence of one who is too precious to forget and who thus needs to be remembered. This child comes along with the grieving parents wherever they go and whatever they do. We said this to the parents earlier: You will get more and more used to the coexistence of play and grief, of work and grief, of holidays and grief, of activities and grief. As caregivers, expect this and affirm it.

When you are out bowling or dancing with your friend and the mood suddenly changes, ask, "Are you thinking of [child's name]?" Even if the answer is no, your guess will be honored as loving. If you choose, you can even be more proactive and ask, prior to the activity, "I know it's been a while since you've been out bowling or dancing. Is there anything I can do to be supportive?"

As for how a grieving parent dresses or appears, we can safely assume you're not likely to say, "Wow, you're really letting yourself go." Is there anything helpful you *can* say? Yes. In a manner similar to what we mentioned with regard to being out together, you could ask, "What have you been thinking and feeling about [child's name] these days?" In short, keep your focus on the grief and not on how it's dressed.

If possible, enjoy and honor the way your grieving friend(s) are being and acting at any given moment, however that is. Try not to be impatient with them, which can imply that you're merely putting up with their grieving until that becomes less prominent and annoying. If they tell you they're tired of their grief, affirm how they are feeling, but don't be too quick to agree with them, say, by suggesting that their grief is tiresome to you, too.

> Grief is at heart about the enduring presence of one who is too precious to forget and who thus needs to be remembered.

We invite you to wonder about whether your friend's grief might be a blessing to you, too. Is there any way that putting yourself out there and risking being vulnerable can benefit you as well as your friend? Recalling the Rumi poem entitled "The Guest House," can you welcome your friend's grief with the faith that even if it feels harsh and challenging, it may be preparing you for some new delight?

Participate in the rituals of grief as you are able or are asked. When asked, treat the invitation as an honor. You must be trusted and special to make that list.

You could make a gift in memory of the child who died. When the charity asks you whether to send a notification to the grieving parent(s), choose "yes" if that squares with your values. Every occasion when the child's name is in print is special. Don't be surprised if you see these notices posted on the fridge at the parent's house.

Finally, as a caregiver, you might sometimes feel as if you're moving toward being a counselor. When the grieving parent talks with you about their grief, empathy is always enough. But what if they start telling you about problems with their partner? And what if this makes you feel uncomfortable? It could be that your felt role seems to be shifting toward counseling. Even if you have the training to do this, the dual role of friend and counselor is still awkward and hard to manage.

In this situation, reflect on whether relationship problems are mentioned frequently or only on occasion. When these problems are mentioned, does your friend vent and move to another topic, or do they grind and grind away at the named problems? And, do you sense that your friend's venting is helping to resolve or entrench the problems being named?

It is fine to set boundaries around topics of conversation that seem counterproductive. It's also fine to suggest that counseling may be helpful to your friend. There are many good resources.

Teaching about good communication and doing marriage counseling are not caregiver responsibilities, but that doesn't prevent you from speaking to the benefit of these skills and support. And if you have received some marriage counseling yourself, you might at least disclose how that was helpful to you and your partner. This could help remove or lessen the stigma of counseling as something people do when they are really messed up and incompetent. How wrong that notion is, and how unfortunate it is for those who could benefit from help!

As has likely been necessary in the course of your friend's grieving, part of your job is to be present to whatever comes up. In some ways, your good listening normalizes your friend's experiences. The fact that you aren't shocked or avoiding them means that they and the experiences they are having are not odd or frightening or somehow below average. Suggest counseling if you feel it could benefit your friend. Frame it as an option for good self-care. You can be a powerful advocate for your friend just by listening well.

## For Reflection and Discussion

### *For Bereaved Parents*

1 How is your grief changing as the weeks and months go by? Are you recognizing any shifts?

2 How are you answering some of the "going public" questions posed early in this chapter?

3 Just for this moment in time, picture your grief in the form of a special event you are planning to attend. How will you get ready for this event, and how will you dress for it?

4 How has grief affected the way you communicate? In particular, how has grief changed the way you talk about your feelings, listen to others, and/or engage conflict?

5 What is one thing you have done to remember your child that could become a ritual of remembrance you repeat in the years ahead?

## *For Caregivers*

1 Take a read on your own grief about this child's loss. Is the support you are offering also supporting you in your grief? If not, what might you do to take care of yourself and your own grief?

2 Reflect on the grief you are observing in your friend. How is it like and not like other grieving experiences you have had?

3 Who or what might you be grieving in your own life (e.g., the death of a grandparent, the loss of a job or sought-after promotion, a long-held dream that has died)? How might your friend's grief help you grieve your own losses?

4 What do you most admire about your friend who is grieving? Do you sense that this admiration is inviting you to develop a similar quality? If so, how might you work on that for yourself?

## Resources

### *Articles*

Devine, Megan. "Get Support." Refuge in Grief, http://www. refugeingrief.com/shop/.

> The infographics on this web page are helpful for those grieving and those who are supporting them.

Empty Arms Bereavement Support. "Rituals." 2017, http://www. emptyarmsbereavement.org/rituals/.

> The organization's website includes support ideas for those whose children have died. This page includes broad-ranging suggestions for developing rituals of remembrance.

Frogge, Stephanie. "The Myth of Divorce Following the Death of Child." Tragedy Assistance Program for Survivors (TAPS), March 1, 2015, https://tinyurl.com/ycfyqaor.

This article looks at the impact of grief on marriage.

Smith, Emily Esfahani. "In Grief, Try Personal Rituals." *The Atlantic*, March 14, 2014, https://tinyurl.com/yates5ef.

This article reports on ritual's helpful effect on the grieving process.

*Books*

Levang, Elizabeth, and Sherokee Ilse. *Remembering with Love: Messages of Hope for the First Year of Grieving and Beyond*. Minneapolis: Fairview, 1992.

The authors provide daily reflections for the first year of bereavement.

Wile, Daniel B. *After the Honeymoon: How Conflict Can Improve Your Relationship*. New York: Wiley, 1988.

Wile's premise is that conflict is inherent in relationships and that the willingness to manage it is a sign and skill of intimacy.

# 5

# Who Am I Becoming?

THE TITLE for this chapter is inspired by the work we did with a grief counselor after our daughter died. Like many parents experiencing grief for the first time, we wondered when our life would get back to normal. Because you have been reading this book, you know you won't return to the old normal, but we didn't have that understanding or perspective at first. In her gentle yet instructive manner, our counselor proposed that instead of asking "When is my life going to get back to normal?" we ask, "Who am I becoming through this process of grief?"

This new question shifted our perspective from wondering how long grief would dominate our emotional landscape to engaging grief as a mysterious but important companion in our emotional and spiritual development. It's easy to think of grief as something that happens *to* you. This question—who am I becoming?—instead sees grief as a force that is waking you, stirring you, leading you deeper into life's fullness. Therefore, rather than wishing grief away, we became more and more inclined to ask, "What, Grief, do you have to show or teach me?"

David found it helpful to do one more thing with this question: he dedicated his becoming to our daughter Erin. David still thinks about his becoming as a kind of living tribute to our daughter. He is who he is because of Erin, who was part of his life and who remains part of his life. Many people, of course, have played significant roles in his becoming, most notably Catherine and our two living daughters. But a deep gratitude and love remains for Erin, without whom his life could not have become what it is.

## Grief in Many Forms

We have come to understand that grief appears in many forms:

1. In the first few days and months after a child's death, we imagine grief appearing in the form of a mighty storm capable of ripping through life and leaving it in shambles. Grief in this form looks terrifying and bewildering (as described in chapter 1).

2. At some point, the numbness begins to ease, and then grief takes the form of emotional intensity and complexity. We experience this form of grief through a myriad of feelings, some familiar and some not (chapter 2).

3. As we move deeper into the first year, grief appears in its vastness—like an ocean we could drown in. Grief in this form looks like it goes on forever. As a result, our attention and energy are focused simply on keeping our head above water (chapter 3).

4. As anniversaries come and go, grief begins to take on the form of remembering and reordering (of priorities, activities, and relationships). We start to sort through the pieces of our life that "stormy grief" scattered everywhere and begin to reassemble our life. Grief in this form appears to be calling us to decide what to keep, what to toss, when and how to remember, and who to help us with these tasks (chapter 4).

5. Eventually, grief will emerge in the form of a catalyst for new life. And this "new life" is not just a patched and scraped-together, impoverished and forever-damaged version of our former life. Rather, it is (or is becoming) a vibrant, authentic, resilient, honest, and redeemed-beyond-our-imagination version of our former life (chapter 5).

New life, however, does not just *show up* as some form of cosmic or godly reward for all you've been through. Instead, new life

> What, Grief, do you have to show or teach me?

emerges as your spirit accepts grief's company and you choose to work toward new life and lean into God's promise of blessing. At this stage, grief can appear to be an agent of God's mercy, love, and redemption.

Grief's transformation parallels your own transformation and growth over the course of a lifetime. Who you are becoming is itself a wonder of interaction between your thoughts and feelings, your beliefs and values, your choices and actions, your perspectives and habits, your experiences, and a host of relationships. Before your child died, you might not have spent much energy reflecting on your own growth and becoming, but grief is now calling you to this holy work.

## Becoming

No one would fault you for choosing the path of least resistance or for wanting your life after the death of a child to be smooth and without roadblocks. You've done enough heavy lifting, right? The early days were hard enough. Turning with intention to your own ongoing growth and the invitation to look under every stone in your emotional, social, and spiritual life may just sound like more suffering. Why follow that path?

### Not an Easy Path

We believe that we are all growing and becoming anyway. We are bombarded daily by cultural messages that suggest subtly or not so subtly that we could use some adjusting, that we're not quite good enough just as we are. This message can be as benign as implying that you're not as happy as you *could* be. It can be as damaging as suggesting that people are not likely to love you if you don't lose weight, look more stylish, become more fit, drink the right beer, drive nicer cars, and the like.

These messages are almost always accompanied by a solution to your problems—a promise of life-enhancing and enriching results that, coincidentally, can be easily and painlessly purchased or

New life emerges as your spirit accepts grief's company and you choose to work toward new life and lean into God's promise of blessing.

achieved. Solutions that appear to be easy are a tempting alternative to grief's seemingly arduous path of becoming.

Our vulnerability to the idea that we need to be better than we are is part of being human. Even Adam and Eve felt the need to be better versions of themselves. They chafed against the limitations they felt (don't eat from that tree!). Based on their behavior, we can see that they must have believed that the life they were living was not quite enough. And they were tempted by the revelation that simply eating a piece of fruit from that one forbidden tree could make them happier and wiser—more like God.

People sometimes blame Adam and Eve for the seemingly ruinous consequences of their action, not just for them, but for us as well. But there is more to their story, and much of it is very instructive to those pondering the path(s) they will choose in their process of becoming.

Douglas John Hall, a pastor of the United Church in Canada and emeritus professor of theology at McGill University, proposed a pertinent idea about Adam and Eve in his book *God and Human Suffering*. Hall wrote that even in the garden of Eden, supposedly idyllic, the first people knew loneliness, limitation, temptation, and anxiety. Hall pointed out that Adam and Eve resisted God's restriction on the Tree of the Knowledge of Good and Evil. They ate the fruit of that very tree, even after they had been instructed not to. This revealed that they were experiencing a sense of incompleteness. If they could be like God, why wouldn't they want to? Though they likely could not have verbalized this desire, they wanted to exceed the limits of their creaturehood. Interestingly, this desire also reveals a worry about whether God was trustworthy.[1]

Hall suggests that even in the garden, Adam and Eve experienced suffering. And after Hall discusses suffering throughout the history of the world, he says, "There is something about a significant portion of the suffering through which we pass that belongs to the very foundation of being—something without which our human being would not and could not be what it is meant to be."[2]

There is something about a significant portion of the suffering through which we pass that belongs to the very foundation of being— something without which our human being would not and could not be what it is meant to be.

Hall's proposal that suffering is foundational to our being runs counter to much popular thought that views suffering as foreign, an intrusion that randomly enters our world and inflicts damage on those in its path. When we think of suffering as being like a foreign intruder, however, the story we tell about our lives will tend to center around how unlucky we were to have it show up in our path. But if we choose to think of suffering as part of our human condition, our story will tend to center around the way we choose to respond to the suffering we have experienced. This is similar to Viktor Frankl's insight as he labored under the severe conditions of a Nazi concentration camp (see chapter 3).

Hall proposed that suffering can actually serve our becoming. He writes, "Through it [suffering]—and *only* through it—our lives are integrated. We become more truly whole, unified, and centered persons. Such suffering is a means—an indispensable means—to our greater appropriation of the *life* that is our birthright as covenant partners of the Lord and Giver of Life."[3]

It is important to also offer this qualification: Hall did not propose that God inflicts suffering on us, nor does Hall see that every form of suffering serves life. For example, torture and abuse clearly do not serve life. Hall did propose that God always *purposes* or redeems suffering so that it eventually serves our becoming.

This final point from Hall addresses the question of whether becoming has to be hard. Hall writes, "The temptation of Everyman and Everywoman [like Adam and Eve] is to *have* their being rather than having to *receive* it, daily, like the manna of the wilderness or

Recall the story of Joseph in the final chapters of Genesis. At the hands of his brothers, he fell into slavery in a foreign land. He spent years languishing in prison, having been falsely accused in palace intrigue. Eventually, he was released and his gifts recognized with responsibility and a rise to power. God redeemed Joseph's suffering; Joseph was transformed from a self-aggrandizing adolescent into a wise and forgiving leader. In the end, he was reconciled with his brothers and reunited with his father. He became a great blessing for many (Genesis 37 and 39–50).

the 'daily bread' of Jesus' model prayer. It is the temptation to possess being rather than to trust the One who gives us our being, daily."[4]

In other words, becoming is not a commodity that can be purchased or achieved. More specifically, our becoming is not served by possessing more clothes, cars, health, wealth, popularity, and the like. That easier path, while commonly traveled, has little to teach us, and its "riches" cannot provide any kind of deep, lasting satisfaction or nurture. Instead, we have an invitation from grief to take the less traveled path. Grief helps us see with unusual clarity what's important in life, and it is on that path that we can reconnect to ourselves and those we love, who are also becoming as they recover.

### Rethinking You

The feelings of vulnerability that come with grief can reveal things about ourselves that we've not noticed before or didn't have the time or energy to address. The death of a child can bring up lots of questions about whether we are equipped to be parents and, ultimately, whether we deserved to be parents in the first place. Because these kinds of questions are normal responses to the death of a child, part of recovery is to come to love ourselves just as we are, in spite of these questions, and just as important, to love others for who they are. In this way, grief exposes some emotional development that most of us need to do as we mature.

Unfortunately, our culture targets us with advertising that generally rests on the premise that we first need to improve or fix some aspect of ourselves in order to be lovable. It's highly likely that you have internalized some of these messages along with similar messages from others who haven't yet learned this important life lesson. As you work to put together the pieces of your new normal, a central task of becoming is to uncover and replace these conditional messages with those that can serve you better. If you want to be a better and more lovable version of yourself, you (ironically) need to work at accepting and loving yourself just as you are.

Grief helps us see with unusual clarity what's important in life, and it is on that path that we can reconnect to ourselves and those we love, who are also becoming as they recover.

> If you want to be a better and more lovable version of yourself, you (ironically) need to work at accepting and loving yourself just as you are.

This kind of self-love is harder to learn than it looks. You may have discovered in your grieving that shame is influencing your life. In our culture, this is true for most of us. Shame is the felt experience of being defective—a conviction that something is wrong with you that cannot be fixed. Shame prompts you to say to yourself, "I'm too needy, too impulsive, too restless, too ugly, too fat, too boring." Shame invites you to view these aspects of self as "defects." And it leaves you with two choices: either try to hide your defects or perform so magnificently that others don't notice them.

Shame gets its power from masquerading as truth. However, you are not defective, and your negative self-talk is no more than a bad habit you have yet to quit.

We may have been taught shame well, and we may have practiced it for years, but we can recover. We give this habit of negative self-talk power and preserve its momentum when we listen to and believe its critical messages. Conversely, we dismantle and reform this habit when we replace the self-critical messages of shame with affirmations that provide positive inspiration and motivation.

> You are not defective, and your negative self-talk is no more than a bad habit you have yet to quit.

When we are attentive to the messages that inform our becoming, we will also likely notice the messages we receive from others. We can use the same discipline with messages we receive from others

Thinkers like Brené Brown and John Bradshaw have written wonderfully helpful books about shame, so do seek out wisdom like theirs if it seems helpful. Both Bradshaw and Brown are *New York Times* best-selling authors and have video presentations available on the Web.

John Bradshaw's (1933–2016) work grew out of his life as an educator and counselor. He wrote several books, among them *Healing the Shame that Binds You*. He hosted a number of PBS specials on addiction, particularly "Bradshaw: On the Family."

Brené Brown's work was referenced in chapter 1. She is a professor at the University of Houston doing qualitative research on shame and vulnerability. She holds the Huffington Foundation–Brené Brown Endowed Chair at the Graduate College of Social Work, University of Houston. To learn more about her work, visit her website, https://brenebrown.com.

as we do for self-talk. Are these messages ones you want to retain or discard? Sometimes these messages will feel warm or affirming. Obviously, keep those. Or they may represent a boundary someone is setting with you. For example, suppose you are managing your own shame fairly well, and you hear someone say to you, "I don't do well with smoking, so if you need to smoke, I would ask you not to do it in my house or car." You could experience this as a well-intended and appropriate boundary.

In contrast to that example, you'll also encounter people who will criticize how you look, dress, feel, talk, or act. If the person offering this criticism is someone you trust, you may choose to take from it what is helpful. However, this kind of criticism also often comes with hidden messages that imply, "This is for your own good," and "No one could ever love you but me." Sometimes another person tells you exactly what's wrong with you and how you're not measuring up, and history says they want you to feel that it's your fault they don't treat you well. When that happens, you might want to seriously question whether this is a kind of "love" that is good for you.

The more we learn to love ourselves, the more we will seek out others whose love for us feels nurturing and supportive. Slowly, we'll learn to create and enforce boundaries with those who can't or don't. Setting boundaries can include speaking up (for example, saying, "I don't like it when you criticize me") or limiting contact with these people.

True self-love, however, is not simply about how well we love ourselves and others love us. While this is a very good and important concern, true self-love invites us also to monitor our way of loving others.

Notice how well you love others just as they are. Notice when you are critical of others, including the aspects of their lives you tend to criticize most. Notice how well you respect others' boundaries and how often you rationalize something you did by thinking it was for the other's own good.

Parallel processes are going on here. We can practice loving ourselves just as we are by loving ourselves as we are. And we can practice loving ourselves just as we are by loving others just as they are. Whenever we are working on one or the other, we are growing our capacity to love self and others fully and with fewer and fewer conditions attached.

There is no clock; there are no mile markers, no winners and losers in this process of becoming. You set the pace. You choose the course. You decide how to reward yourself for accomplishments along the way—when to rest and when to dive back in. Some days, you will engage this work halfheartedly and plod along at a snail's pace. That is fine. Other days, you'll feel full of energy and passion. That's fine, too.

Grief opens a door to making the process of becoming a way of life. It's what we do today. It's what we make of today. It's how we look at today. When we who grieve look ahead, we know only too well that plans are only hopes for the future, not guarantees of it. When we look back, it's to learn from what we have experienced, rather than longing for things to be different from the way they are. Becoming keeps its eyes on today as the one and only day we are given to think and do and be and say what has the best potential to bless our own lives and the lives of those we love. And becoming

True self-love invites us also to monitor our way of loving others.

not only sees that this is all we have control over, but also trusts that everything we need is present in this very day.

### Finding Your Center

One common way to think of yourself is in terms of the roles you play. At home, you are a parent and possibly also a partner (or spouse). At work, you have a job title and set of responsibilities to go with it. To some, you are a friend, a teammate, or mentor. Roles like these provide structure and definition to your life.

These roles also come with expectations. Children have ideas about what kind of parent they want you to be. Spouses or partners have a similar set of ideas, as do friends and colleagues and teammates. For example, people often speak of *faithful* spouses, *loyal* friends, *unselfish* teammates, and *hardworking* colleagues. Children, too, speak of having *great* moms or *bossy* moms or *always-busy* moms. Even advertising gets into the game—for example, "*Choosy* mothers choose Jif." Bottom line: when you assume a role, someone will always want to rate how well you are doing in it.

And here's the further rub: people throughout history have been playing these roles. So it's inevitable that how you perform (for example, in the role of parent) will be compared with how others have performed in that role. Mothers can look to Mary, the mother of Jesus; our own grandmothers and mother; the celebrity "super moms" we see in media; and even someone like Mother Theresa, a mother to the poor. While their example might inspire and guide our own parenting, it can feel impossible to live up to the standards set by these mothers, especially in aggregate.

Since much of your becoming gets filtered through these roles you play, you need some strategy for choosing a path. We learned a simple rhetorical twist that helps clarify the dynamic at work here. A lifelong friend of David's once wrote down the same words but with different emphases: "David is a *pastor*" and "*David* is a pastor." The idea implicit in this exercise is true for everyone. Will we be defined by the roles we play based on other's expectations of the

Becoming keeps its eyes on today as the one and only day we are given to think and do and be and say what has the best potential to bless our own lives and the lives of those we love.

roles? Or will we bring our own gifts, strengths, faith, passion, instincts, and values to the roles we inhabit?

The difference between the two is significant. If we take on the expectations of others, then we need to constantly learn what is expected of us in the roles we play and must continually strive to meet those expectations—whether or not we have the gifts, skills, interest, or passion to do so. The second point of view assumes that the world needs us to be who we are and that each of us, as a package deal, matters.

Grief may be forcing you to renegotiate your self-understanding, especially around the roles you hold. Is it OK to be a parent struggling with grief over the loss of your child, or do you need to keep a stiff upper lip and not let it slow you down? If a stiff upper lip is where you tend to default, what happens when you just can't meet that standard? What happens to your sense of yourself when the tears come unbidden or the dishes just can't get done? What if you can't focus enough for this presentation? What if you don't have the energy to hold up another in their suffering? What happens if you need to lean on someone else's faith because yours just doesn't make sense to you anymore?

> Grief may be forcing you to renegotiate your self-understanding.

## Thoughts about Self-Care

Try this out for yourself. First, write your name, and then in uppercase letters, write a role you fill—for example, parent, spouse/partner, friend, or your job title. Second, write your name in all uppercase letters; next to it, write the role.

Now notice: Do you feel the freedom to be a parent, spouse, friend, or worker *simply by being who you are?* Or do you feel the need to live up to some kind of ideal archetypal definition of this role?

Now try out this exercise using the role "child of God." There are plenty of biblical role models: Ruth, Moses, Peter, and Tabitha. There are also people you have known or know of (living or dead) who you see as pillars of faith. Do you tend to define your role as a child of God based on the example set by others or as simply the call to be who you are?

The gospel says that God's love for us is without condition, that we were made on purpose. We are not a fluke but have been created by God with gifts and a rich palate of emotions to help us interpret this world that God has created. On those days when you are off your game, you are not of less value than the days when you feel strong and productive. Not from God's' point of view. The challenge is to believe it, especially when we are grieving.

We are proposing that you take this perspective: God, through your experience of grief, is calling forth your own inner spirit/teacher. And it is this inner teacher who is leading you deeper and deeper into the richness and mystery of life, to a place where joy and sorrow live side by side, so you can be fully you and love yourself for it. This is the gift of becoming—for you, your partner, your children, and the world.

## Parenting Surviving Children

If you have surviving children who need you to be a parent, or if you decide to have another baby, you will face the challenges of parenting in grief. Your children need your very best, but the best version of you might not be always be available while you are grieving. This is simply true and understandable and forgivable. And it's true that you likely also have been reminded by the loss of your child just how precious and priceless these little ones are. So how to give them your best?

There are many wonderful books on parenting, and it would go far beyond the scope of this book to attempt to capture and distill even a small part of that wisdom here. So instead, we'll look at parenting from the perspective of how it serves your becoming. You cannot engage parenting without seeing a reflection of yourself in the process.

Early in David's parenting, our surviving twin at age five wanted to swim in our kiddie pool in the backyard while still wearing her clothes. It was hot! David's instinctive response was to say no. Then Cara

> On those days when you are off your game, you are not of less value than the days when you feel strong and productive. Not from God's' point of view.

> God, through your experience of grief, is calling forth your own inner spirit/teacher.

asked, "Why not?" Prior to her sister's death, he might have reasoned that his parents would have said no or that swimming pools (of any size) demand that one wear a swimming suit. However, grief had taught him something, and he thought, "Her clothes are all cotton. They are colorfast and will eventually get thrown into the wash, where they will get plenty wet. Furthermore, she is excited to get into the pool now, and it might just feel novel and fun to do so in her clothes and not in a swimsuit." In his becoming, he discovered a new answer to her request: "Yes."

Parenting provides a most excellent environment in which to practice becoming. Parenting tests the limits of our patience, demands incredible energy and stamina, calls for endless creativity and resourcefulness, and is a never-ending process of boundary setting. Parenting gives us thousands and thousands of chances to practice loving ourselves and our children just as they are.

*Vulnerable Parent*

Two aspects of parenting while grieving bear special mention. The first of these is vulnerability. You have experienced the death of a child and are more aware than you want to be that children can die. Since they are mortal like you, their lives are similarly precarious. They can succumb to illness or be killed in accident. How do grieving parents figure out what to do with this hyperconsciousness about life's precariousness and the accompanying feelings of vulnerability?

One response to vulnerability is to become overprotective—hovering over our children and limiting their access to any activity that is too risky. This may help us feel safer, but we could wonder how this might affect them in the long run. Another response is to adopt a mind-set of "what will be is what will be." Though this approach could intensify our feelings of vulnerability, we might choose it if we thought it would free our children from being burdened by our primal worries.

Parenting gives us thousands and thousands of chances to practice loving ourselves and our children just as they are.

Many parents choose some sort of middle ground—a mixture of hovering, safety measures, and letting go. For example, we might hover when our children are swimming and demand they wear a helmet when riding a bike. At the same time, we might allow them to climb on rocks and playground equipment, knowing they will sometimes fall off.

Feelings of vulnerability are there for a reason. They do help us manage safety risks. And they also remind us that life is finite and thus invite us to value this moment with our children as if it could be the last. Parenting gets complicated by feelings of vulnerability, but it also gets enriched by them. Treating each day and each encounter with our children as a precious gift is a marvelous way to engage them.

### Parenting the Vulnerable

It's not unusual for a person to be unaware of a sibling who died, sometimes until adulthood. Perhaps parents who make the choice not to tell want to protect their subsequent children from the pain of grief. Whatever the reason, it's likely these parents made that choice out of love. However, we invite you to tell your children they had a sibling who died, and to do so early and often. We have three reasons for this perspective:

1. Our children will almost certainly sense that our grief is present, whether we tell them or not.
2. Someday our children will also experience grief and will need to know what to do with it.
3. Grief is part of who we are now and is a part of the family story. It can't simply be split off and hidden.

Children are quick to notice their parent's emotions. For example, when they see us crying, they'll almost always say, "Mommy's sad." Or maybe they'll ask about it: "Why is Daddy sad?" If we choose not to tell them why we are sad, they might feel confused.

> Treating each day and each encounter with our children as a precious gift is a marvelous way to engage them.

Children are prone to think they are the source of our feelings, so they often try to do something about those feelings. A child might dance around and make happy faces in order to make us feel happy again. Or they might bring us their blanket or a favorite stuffed animal, thinking maybe it will soothe us. Yet if our sadness persists and we've not helped our children to understand why our grief persists, they might feel a sense of failure and powerlessness to either comfort us or make us feel happy. This is one reason why trying to protect our children from the anguish of our grief can have unintended negative consequences.

Part of our parental task is to help our children learn to manage their own emotions. Emotions simply are a part of life, and they are actually valuable clues to help us interpret our experience of living. So learning to recognize and listen to emotions is an important task, along with the equally valuable task of deciding how to act on them, both in the immediate moment and beyond. Do we need to soothe ourselves, run for the hills, seek shelter, reach out for support, or set a boundary? Imagine being sad and even crying and telling your children that you aren't sad, rather than affirming their awareness of your emotions. Awareness of others' emotions is a vital social skill. Denying your sadness teaches them to mistrust their instincts. In addition, you aren't helping them learn how to manage their own sadness, which is an inevitable part of anyone's life.

A second reason to tell our children about a sibling who died is that they, too, need to learn how to grieve. We might reason that this is something they don't need to learn until they are older. But grief in some form visits us at every stage of life. Judith Viorst, author of *Necessary Losses* (Simon and Schuster, 1986), examines common experiences of grief that occur from birth to death. She proposes, for example, that our first loss is leaving the womb. In the womb, babies experience sustenance, warmth, and comfort, all while being protected from the perils and suffering of the outside world. Once born, they suddenly experience cold, hunger, discomfort, bodily functions, separateness, noise, and so forth.

> Grief in some form visits us at every stage of life.

These childhood losses continue. Children grieve when they lose their blanket or pacifier. They grieve when a pet dies, even if it's just a goldfish. They grieve when a good friend moves away. They even grieve when we tell them they have to leave the playground or when we tell them it's time for bed. They may not understand, as we do, that they can do this again tomorrow, so they might imagine they may never get to do this again.

None of these childhood losses seems to compare in scale or intensity to a parent's experience of the death of a child. Yet it doesn't serve us or our children well to draw too sharp a distinction between their losses and ours. Each loss is real, comes with similar emotions, and requires self-care and support. When we share our experience of grief with our children, we are helping them to understand that *we* are sad and to see how we are taking care of ourselves. We are also helping them to understand their sadness (when they grieve) and to see how they might take care of themselves.

Earlier, we said parenting is like a mirror in which you see your reflection. Here we ask you to notice how your own issues might be revealed in the responses you make to your children's grief. Notice especially when you feel dismissive of it. Maybe you remember being told as a child (when crying about some loss), "Oh, for goodness' sake, don't make a mountain out of a molehill." This might have taught you that it's silly or selfish to grieve some losses—that to do so only garners others' disdain or disapproval— and that it's really true that "there's no use crying over spilled milk."

You can't say to others, "Get over it" without it rising from an internal, personal need to do the same. Yet, when you give time, space, permission, consolation, encouragement, and support to others, no matter what they are grieving, you are very likely to do the same for yourself. And, when you engage your child's grief with patience and respect, your grief is transformed into a gift that allows you to be this sensitive and loving as their parent.

The final reason for telling children about grief is that it's simply part of who you are now and can't be hidden, even if you tried. This is your family story. And why would you try to hide it, given how central it is to your self-understanding and way of being? Though you surely won't choose to share your grief with everyone, you will need to share it with loved ones, because you need their love and understanding. Your children are among those who need to know, because sometimes they will be able to comfort you—another powerful life skill.

Now, practically, how do you talk to your children about your grief and the death of their sibling? Start simply. For example, you might say, "Mommy once had another baby, but they died." You know there is way more to the story than this, but you hold off sharing those details for now. Sometimes, this simple explanation is enough for your child to chew on at the moment. It's likely, however, that sometime later they will ask, "Why did they die?" Again, you keep it simple, maybe saying, "There was something wrong with their heart or lungs." (Use language that describes *your* child's death; tell the truth.)

In time, a surviving sibling is likely to ask more and more questions, and you may sense the child is capable of hearing more details about their sibling's death. When the questions come, take the opportunity to talk to your child not only about their sibling, but also about your feelings of grief. Include your children in rituals of remembrance. Take them with you when you visit the cemetery,

Children need to know that when someone we love dies, it is painful, but death is a very normal part of life.

Some very good children's books can help you talk to children, even very young children, about death. Ask your local librarian for a few suggestions. One author is Judith Viorst, whose specialty is loss and learning through life stages. She has written children's books that acknowledge children's losses. Encourage aunts and uncles and other important adults in your children's life to read these books, too. Helping other loving adults in your children's life learn how to talk about death will normalize this experience of loss. This also helps your child understand that he or she was not the cause or somehow responsible for a sibling's death. Children need to know that when someone we love dies, it is painful, but death is a very normal part of life.

let them light the candle on an anniversary, or have them help you plant a tree in memory of the sibling who has died.

Ask your children how they might like to remember their sibling. These moments can be an opportunity to talk to your children about heaven or an afterlife. Talking about heaven may help children see how faith informs and sustains you in your grief. We don't expect you will have it all figured out, but we know you will be thinking about it. Especially for older children, you can let them in on the wondering you are doing. This sets a great example for them of what it means to be a faith-full adult. You can also talk together with your pastor.

Catherine was pregnant with twins as she entered the fourth and final year of her seminary studies. Among the requirements for graduation and approval for ordination, seniors had to write a paper setting forth a theology of God and life as clearly as possible. She set about to write her paper before the twins arrived, knowing that it would be much harder to find the time once they were born. However, the twins arrived early, five weeks before their due date. Eight weeks later, Erin died unexpectedly.

Following these births and Erin's death, Catherine considered the question of life after death from a new and poignant perspective. The first version of her paper had little to say about this issue. But because of Erin's death, the promise of eternal life and an implied reunion with those we love held a much more prominent place in her landscape of faith. The final version of her paper reflected this newly important belief that she will be reunited with Erin one day.

Some people worry that if their child was not baptized, they will not be granted a place in heaven. The biblical record seems to point toward a reunion with God for all those whom God loves. If God created your little one, and God did, we have to believe that God's embrace will be as sure and reassuring as it is for those whose baptism happened before death came.

The biblical record offers several understandings of heaven and the nature of eternal life. By the time of Jesus, there was growing acceptance of the idea of resurrection, though not all believed in life after death. The Sadducees, for example, did not (Mark 12:18), while the Pharisees did. Christian theologians have wrestled with the question of life after death for centuries, and other religious traditions have as well.

Reports of near-death experiences and other people's stories about sensing the presence of a loved one who recently died all shape our experience of grief and our hopes for reunion with those we have loved and lost. Children may have very specific questions that no one can really answer with confidence from the biblical record—questions like "Will my sister grow up in heaven?" or "Will I recognize her when I get there?" However, faith says we will be with God along with all those God has loved. Respond to children's questions from within their capacity to imagine, trusting that God and the child's own experiences of death will shape an understanding that can support the process of grief.

You never know how being transparent about your grief will play out in the lives of your children. But you can trust it will strengthen the bonds of love in your family and promote your children's capacity to deal with the losses they will face.

We remember a Saturday morning when high-school classmates of our youngest (then age seventeen) started showing up at our house. She was making breakfast for them. We thought this was sweet but then learned they were gathering prior to a funeral service for a classmate who had died suddenly in an accident. Our daughter had arranged this on her own—a response to her own grief and a way of tending to the grief of her friends. We were both proud and touched by this thoughtful response. Our daughter knew something about grief. And this is good.

## Transforming Your Loss into Support for Others

Your eyes have been opened by grief. You know you are not the only parent who has lost a child. Soon, if it hasn't happened already, you'll learn of others who are grieving the death of a child. You are in a unique position to understand and be empathetic. There is much you've learned and much you might want to share that you think could be helpful. The most important thing is that you know the devastation firsthand, and you have survived and, by now, may even sense that you are thriving.

At our first support group meeting, just three days after our daughter's death, we were oddly comforted by the presence of other newly bereaved parents. It was also a little terrifying to think that other babies had died in this mysterious way (SIDS) and so many other parents were trying to come to grips with what had happened. We felt less alone among those other parents, because we were all so vulnerable and lost. Hope, however, came from the pair of parents whose children had died years ago. In them, we glimpsed the possibility that we might survive this intact and find happiness and equilibrium again someday. We remember little of what they said, perhaps because they listened more than they talked, but just their presence was an infusion of normal—a normal we hoped would be ours eventually.

As the years pass, you will become a source of hope for bereaved parents who walk in your footsteps. Your presence will be a sign of hope, because you have walked this path before them and found a new normal that gives your life shape and joy. Though some support group participants are eager to tell newcomers what to do or not to do, you know that teaching and fixing and explaining are rarely helpful to someone who is newly grieving. You can share parts of your story, but only after you have held space open for the holy stories of those in the room whose grief is raw and who are just learning about the new story they will someday tell.

By now, the reality of the loss of your child and your grief has become a constant companion. You will never forget this little one, even if you never had a chance to hold your baby. You became a parent when you surrounded your baby with love. What a blessing that was for your child! And what a blessing for you, in spite of the pain of your loss. We are unbelievably vulnerable in our relationship to our children, whether they die or they live. Yet the gift and privilege of being parents is as breathtaking as it is risky.

Your eyes have been opened by grief.

We have often said that we are grateful for our daughter, and as the years have gone by, we can include her death within our gratitude. We have learned so much, though we always also say, "But we would have been happy to learn those things in any other way." This is the enigmatic nature of grief. It is such an opportunity to mature into a human being who can hold both joy and sorrow with equal appreciation, to move into a more subtle understanding of what it means to live a good life. While we do not wish pain to be the conduit for growth, it seems it just is. We miss our daughter and wonder what life would have been like with three children seated around our table. We will never know that. Instead of focusing on the past, we choose to celebrate the fullness we have received and wonder at the generosity of God's grace to redeem even the most painful time of our life together. Most days, we can do that. Truly, life has risen from death. Thanks be to God.

> While we do not wish pain to be the conduit for growth, it seems it just is.

> Truly, life has risen from death. Thanks be to God.

> The person grieving is living into their grief with God's promise of blessing.

## Caregiver Tips

### Becoming for the Caregiver

You were reminded at the beginning of this chapter that grief appears in many forms. You likely have become familiar with the stormy, oceanic, and intense expressions of grief; even the remembering and reordering of priorities may now seem familiar. But it's likely that the metaphor of becoming is new. Grief is rarely depicted as a force of awakening that leads people deeper into life's fullness.

The change of perspective is to conceive of grief as not just an ongoing process, but also an important and life-giving ongoing process. In other words, grief doesn't linger just because the sadness runs so deep. It lingers also because the person grieving is living into their grief with God's promise of blessing.

Still, this grief work is hard. The tears remain. Other, older losses may come to mind—some of which were never grieved. And some grief fatigue can set in.

The fact that grieving remains hard tempts all parents, at least on occasion, to look for an easier way. This is where your role as caregiver can get tricky. Do you help them stay with the process, or do you agree with them that it's important to take a break now and then? The answer: it depends. If you sense that your friend is doing some really good "becoming work" and needs encouragement to stay with it, then you might encourage them to stay with it. But if you sense they have hit the wall and really do need a break, you can encourage them to take one.

Reread the section called "Finding Your Center" and do the exercise in the sidebar (on page 123), using the role of caregiver.

You are a caregiver and not a counselor. Being a counselor is a different role, one that usually comes with training and certification. That said, caregivers often are able to notice whether a friend is striving to achieve something because it brings joy and satisfaction or because of a felt need to please or live up to another's expectation. Sometimes you can tell the difference between these two kinds of striving by the way your friend talks about it. That is, if your friend is striving for their own sake, you might hear them say, "This is harder than I thought it would be." But, when they are striving to please someone else, they might say instead, "Ugh! I hate all this pressure!"

Sometimes we choose to live up to others' expectations of us. That's not all bad and, in fact, can be necessary. Unfortunately, seeking to meet the expectations of others can become unhealthy if behind this striving is a felt sense that we are not good enough as we are. As a caregiver, try to notice if or when this might be true for your grieving friends. It is always appropriate to look for ways to affirm them as they are, to like them as they are, and to love them as they are.

More specifically, affirm their introspection and reflective process whenever it occurs. Encourage them to keep pondering good questions—say, "How does God redeem suffering?"—and engage these questions with them if you are so inclined. Don't rush to solve the mystery of life for them, but rather let them sink into it and admire them for doing so.

To stay with a person engaged in the process of their becoming, especially when grief is the stimulus, pay attention to your own process of becoming. How is your friend's grief affecting you? How does it cause you to rethink how you are living your own life? Do you too feel the need to perform so others will like you? Do you try to live up to certain role models? How well do you do with accepting and loving yourself just as you are?

Just as your friend's grief is a catalyst for their own becoming, it can also be a catalyst for your becoming. For example, if your friend is exploring shame, wonder if this is a feature of your own life that you might benefit from exploring. If your friend is paying attention to self-talk (especially when it's critical), consider doing the same yourself. If your friend is trying to live one day at a time, see what difference it makes when you do it, too.

The point is not to copy everything your grieving friend is doing. Rather, it is to notice when your friend is doing something that calls to you—that seems like a helpful and timely thing for you to work on, too. There is a saying that "imitation is the sincerest form of flattery." Your friend may sometimes feel like a burden on you when you are always the helper and they are always the one receiving your help. But you will encourage your friend whenever they see you are learning and benefiting from their grief process. In these moments, your friend's grief is transformed from burden into blessing. That's a gift to all.

## Boundaries for Caregivers

Although you have much to learn from your grieving friends, that doesn't mean these friends necessarily need to become the center of your life. Remember that their grief (and their becoming) is vast and ongoing. Consider the part you want to play in it. Consider, too, that the better you get at providing loving support to others, the more requests for that support you might get. So choose the course that's right for you. Set limits that respect your time, energy, other relationships, and priorities. If your friend would like to see you every week, and you feel once a month is the best you can do, stick with once a month. Better to see your friend less often and come with good energy than to see them more often and feel resentful about it.

You might be encouraged to know that Jesus wasn't a caregiver who said yes to everyone all the time. Even Jesus needed to take breaks. The Gospel of Mark tells the story of Jesus going out one morning to a deserted place to pray. His disciples "hunted for him," and "When they found him, they said to him, 'Everyone is searching for you'" (Mark 1:36–37). One implication of the disciples' words is this question: Why are you here when everyone needs you? One implication of Jesus's behavior is this response: I'm here because, like you, I need my downtime.

We're glad you've been reading this book. You have learned some ways to be supportive to others in their grief and also ways to befriend your own grief (related to the losses you have experienced). We've erred on the side of giving you more information than you can take in all at once. Use whatever you've found helpful, and practice it in a manner that's right for you. Thank you for accompanying us and your grieving friends on this path. It is holy work.

> Even Jesus needed to take breaks.

## For Reflection and Discussion

### *For Bereaved Parents*

1  How would you describe your process of becoming thus far? What is this process inviting you to explore or do next?

2  Think of a recent time when you were tempted to seek or choose a quick fix, even when you knew it wouldn't really solve the problem you were facing. What made this quick fix so tempting, and why?

3  What does your "garden of Eden" look like? How does wishing for life to be like this affect you (for good and for ill)?

4 What is the main obstacle for you in accepting and loving yourself just as you are? What might it take to find a way around this obstacle?

5 Consider the role(s) that are most important to you. How have you shaped these roles to fit who you are? What shaping work, do you think, still remains? And what will your next steps be?

## *For Caregivers*

Reflect on the same questions suggested for bereaved parents in this chapter.

## Resources

### *Articles and Videos*

Brown, Brené. *Listening to Shame.* TED Talk, March 2012, https://tinyurl.com/ngtbqqp.

> Brown talks about how shame shows up in everyday life and suggests how to disarm it.

Reece, Tamekia. "When a Child's Sibling Dies," *Parents*, https://tinyurl.com/yb5v5ntb

> This article is not specifically about the loss of a pregnancy or early infant death, but rather offers a general look at working with children's own sense of grief.

Rodriguez, Jodie. "Book Lists: Talking to Children about Death of a Sibling," Growing Book by Book, November 17, 2014, https://tinyurl.com/y7dovtet.

> This article lists and describes books to help in in the case of miscarriage or early infant loss.

Schott, Judith, and Alix Henley. *Supporting Children When a Baby Has Died.* Sands, November 2013, https://tinyurl.com/ybraaafx.

A booklet from a UK charity dedicated to stillbirth and neonatal death. Especially helpful are chapters dealing with children of different ages.

## Books

### FOR ADULTS

Bradshaw, John. *Healing the Shame That Binds You.* Rev. ed. Deerfield Beach, FL: Health Communications, 2005.

Bradshaw offers a diagnosis of shame, focusing on its origins and effects, and then provides exercises effective for discarding shame's unhelpful messages and adopting healing affirmations.

Brown, Brené. *The Gifts of Imperfection.* Center City, MN: Hazelden, 2010.
———. *The Gifts of Imperfect Parenting.* Audio CD, unabridged ed. Sounds True, 2013.

Brown provides suggestions and encouragement for those who want to reclaim and affirm inborn gifts and callings and not simply respond to the expectations of others.

Hall, Douglas John. *God and Human Suffering: An Exercise in the Theology of the Cross.* Minneapolis: Augsburg, 1986.

Hall writes for pastors and seminary students, but his language is accessible to a much wider audience. For those who are spiritually inclined, this is an insightful book about how we might understand and engage human suffering.

Nadeau, Janice Winchester. *Families Making Sense of Death.* Thousand Oaks, CA: Sage, 1997.

Nadeau's research on how families create meaning for a death explores a range of responses.

Viorst, Judith. *Necessary Losses.* New York: Simon and Schuster, 1986.

> Viorst examines common losses experienced from the moment of birth until our death. Her insights help us acknowledge and grieve these losses so we can embrace what's next in life free from unresolved grief(s).

FOR CHILDREN

Hanson, Warren. *The Next Place.* Minneapolis: Waldman House, 1997.

> Vivid graphics and nature scenes accompany words that imagine the "next place" we go to after we die.

Viorst, Judith. *The Tenth Good Thing about Barney.* New York: Aladdin Paperbacks, 1971.

> A boy remembers ten good things about his cat after it dies.

# Notes

### Chapter 1: How Can This Have Happened?

1. The RSA, "Brené Brown on Empathy," RSA Shorts, YouTube, December 10, 2013, https://tinyurl.com/qbvwd2y.
2. Brené Brown, "The Power of Vulnerability," TEDxHouston, June 2010, https://tinyurl.com/k5y5k2d.

### Chapter 2: Why Do I Feel like This?

1. For more, see Jon Kabat-Zinn's biography page at the University of Massachusetts Medical School and the Center for Mindfulness in Medicine, Health Care, and Society, https://tinyurl.com/y9ppyymx.
2. Coleman Barks, trans., *The Essential Rumi* (HarperSanFrancisco, 1995), 109.
3. Co-Active Coaching is a model for life coaching in which both David and Catherine have trained. There are many other models, but the idea of open-ended questions is common among them. For more information, see "Why Co-Active Training?" on the website of the Coaches Training Institute, https://tinyurl.com/ybxeeqpp.
4. For a brief summary of these ideas, see the introduction in Harold S. Kushner, *When Bad Things Happen to Good People*, anniversary ed. (New York: Schocken, 2001).

### Chapter 3: How Do I Keep Going?

1. Sermon by Sheldon Tostengard (1935–2012), professor of homiletics at Luther Seminary in St. Paul, Minnesota, delivered at Our Saviour's Lutheran Church, December 4, 1984. For more on Tostengard, see https://tinyurl.com/ydagv3es.
2. Stephen Mitchell, ed., *The Selected Poetry of Rainer Maria Rilke* (New York: Vintage International, 1989), 205, 207.

3. Mary Malotky, portions of a letter sent from a Peace Corps assignment in the highlands of Papua New Guinea, December 1984.

4. "Persistent depressive disorder (dysthymia)," Mayo Clinic, August 8, 2017, https://www.mayoclinic.org/diseases-conditions/persistent-depressive-disorder/symptoms-causes/syc-20350929. Used with permission of Mayo Foundation for Medical Education and Research. All rights reserved.

5. William A. Barry, *God and You: Prayer as a Personal Relationship* (Mahway, NJ: Paulist, 1985), chap. 5.

## Chapter 4: What Do I Make of Life after This?

1. Jean Galica, "The Effects of the Death of a Child on a Marriage," Theravive, https://tinyurl.com/yanndof7.

2. New York: Wiley, 1988.

3. Martin Luther, Apology of the Augsburg Confession, Article XIII, The Sacraments 211.3, in Theodore G. Tappert, trans. and ed., *The Book of Concord* (Philadelphia: Fortress Press, 1959).

4. Luther, Large Catechism, Lord's Supper 454.68, in Tappert, *The Book of Concord*.

5. In *Slamming Open the Door* (Farmington, ME: Alice James, 2009).

## Chapter 5: Who Am I Becoming?

1. Douglas John Hall, *God and Human Suffering* (Minneapolis: Augsburg, 1986), 54–55.

2. Hall, *God and Human Suffering*, 57.

3. Hall, *God and Human Suffering*, 65.

4. Hall, *God and Human Suffering*, 81.